CW01523639

THE

SOUTH

ISLAND

(New Zealand)

TRAVEL GUIDE

TABLE OF CONTENT

WELCOME TO

SOUTH ISLAND
(NEW ZEALAND)

TRAVEL GUIDE

Copyright © 2023 by **Nellie E. Hartley**

All rights reserved.

No part of this Non-fiction publication may be reproduced or transmitted in any form or by any means, including photocopying, recording, or other electronic methods, without the prior permission of the publisher, except in the case of brief quotations embodied in critical reviews and certain other non-commercial uses permitted by copyright law.

This publication is designed to provide accurate and authoritative information regarding the subject matter covered. It is sold with the understanding that the publisher does not render legal, accounting, or other professional services. If legal advice or other expert assistance is required, the services of a competent professional person should be sought.

GETTING STARTED

Introduction

South Island, New Zealand stands as an unparalleled treasure in a world adorned with breath-taking landscapes. Located in the southern expanse of the Pacific, this captivating land calls out to adventurers from far and wide, enticing them with its irresistible charm. From the majestic peaks of the Southern Alps to the unspoiled fjords, from the untamed coastline to the lush valleys, South Island reveals a tapestry of wonders that awaken the senses and ignite the spirit.

Each step taken on this extraordinary island unfolds a journey of discovery, immersing visitors in a symphony of natural marvels. Prepare to be spellbound by the magnificence of Aoraki/Mount Cook, where lofty summits pierce the heavens and glaciers carve their path through rugged valleys. Stand in awe of the ethereal allure of Milford Sound, where mist-wreathed cliffs descend into serene waters, and cascading waterfalls paint a picture of sheer grandeur. The landscapes of South Island epitomize the immense power and graceful elegance of Mother Nature.

As you venture deeper into this enchanted realm, you will encounter a wealth of unique flora and fauna. South Island boasts one of the most pristine ecosystems on Earth, harbouring endemic species found nowhere else. Keep a keen eye out for the playful antics of the rare Hector's dolphins as they frolic in the shimmering turquoise waters. Delight in the graceful flight of the endangered kiwi bird, an emblem of national pride, as it scampers through dense forests. In this land of captivating biodiversity, every moment offers a glimpse into the wonders of evolution and the interconnectedness of life.

Yet, South Island is not merely a feast for the eyes but a playground for thrill-seekers and outdoor enthusiasts. Strap on your hiking boots and embark on epic journeys along world-renowned trails, such as the Milford Track or the Abel Tasman Coast Track. Traverse untamed landscapes, crossing ancient forests, emerald lakes, and untouched alpine meadows. Feel your adrenaline surge as you partake in heart-pounding adventures like bungee jumping, skydiving, or jet boating. South Island's realm of adventure promises an exhilarating experience for all who embrace its challenges.

Beyond its natural wonders, South Island is also a haven for a vibrant and welcoming culture. Encounter the warmth of the Kiwi spirit as you engage with the locals, whose easy-going charm and genuine hospitality create cherished connections.

Share conversations over a glass of acclaimed Marlborough wine or relish the flavours of fresh seafood from the abundant Southern Ocean. Let yourself be captivated by the rich heritage of the Māori people, whose traditions and stories resonate through the land, infusing it with a profound sense of spirituality.

As you uncover the chapters of your South Island odyssey, you will reveal a harmonious symphony of captivating experiences. Let the allure of this extraordinary land guide you on a voyage of a lifetime, where nature's splendour, thrilling adventures, and heartfelt encounters intertwine to create an unforgettable tapestry of discovery. With every passing moment on South Island, the allure of its natural wonders and the warmth of its people become more intoxicating, drawing you deeper into its embrace. The island's pristine wilderness, untamed and unspoiled, evokes a sense of timelessness as if you have stepped into a realm untouched by the rush of modern life.

Immerse yourself in the serenity of Fiordland, where the ancient fjords loom like cathedral walls, their reflective waters mirroring the majesty above. Here, silence is profound, broken only by the occasional cry of a distant bird or the gentle lapping of water against the shore. As you cruise through these serene waterways, a feeling of tranquillity washes over you, and you can't help but be moved by the sheer magnitude of nature's artistry.

The adventure-seekers among you will find solace in the rugged landscapes of the West Coast. Brace yourself as you traverse the imposing Franz Josef and Fox glaciers, behemoths of ice that seem to defy gravity as they inch their way downward. Feel the thrill of exploration as you venture into the heart of lush rainforests, where ancient ferns and moss-covered trees create an otherworldly atmosphere, reminiscent of a primordial age.

South Island's dynamic landscapes do not end there. Journey to the east, and you'll discover the enchanting Canterbury Plains, a patchwork of rolling hills and golden fields that stretch to meet the distant horizon. Nestled amidst this vast expanse, you'll find the vibrant city of Christchurch, a testament to the resilience of its people after the devastating earthquakes that shaped its modern identity.

Travel south, and the pristine shores of the Otago Peninsula beckon you. Home to diverse wildlife, including the adorable yellow-eyed penguin and the royal albatross, it is a haven for bird enthusiasts and photographers alike. A visit to the charming city of Dunedin unveils its Scottish heritage, evident in its architecture, traditions, and the warm-hearted hospitality of its residents.

No journey to South Island would be complete without delving into the surreal landscapes of Queenstown and Wanaka. Here, adrenaline and beauty coalesce, as you find yourself torn between heart-pounding adventure and the temptation to simply bask in the stunning alpine scenery. Ski down powdery slopes in winter or feel the rush of skydiving as you soar over turquoise lakes and emerald valleys.

As your exploration nears its conclusion, you'll find yourself yearning for more time on this remarkable island. South Island, New Zealand, is not just a destination; it's an unforgettable experience, a place where every moment is etched into the fabric of your soul.

So, let this be an invitation, an enticement to embark on an extraordinary adventure, where the wonders of nature and the warm embrace of its people converge. As you turn the pages of your South Island journey, let your heart be captivated, and your spirit forever touched by the enchanting beauty of this island paradise. Let South Island, New Zealand, welcome you with open arms, for it is a land where dreams are made and memories are crafted, waiting eagerly for you to add your chapter to its rich tapestry.

My First Time Visit

As the plane touched down in Christchurch, my heart swelled with anticipation. I had heard tales of the South Island's mesmerizing beauty, and now, finally, I stood at the gateway to this enchanting realm. Excitement coursed through my veins as I embarked on a journey that promised to be nothing short of extraordinary.

Welcome to my world of wonder and discovery as I take you on an enthralling adventure through the untamed landscapes and captivating allure of South Island, New Zealand. From the moment I set foot on its shores for the first time, I was immediately entranced by the majestic Southern Alps, their snow-capped peaks reaching towards the heavens, beckoning me to explore further. Each step I took unveiled a new surprise from cascading glaciers to turquoise waters igniting a fire of excitement within me.

Join me in the coastal haven of marine wonders, Kaikoura, where the dance of whales and the playful acrobatics of dolphins left me spellbound. The sight of albatrosses soaring gracefully above the ocean was a symphony of wings against the endless blue sky, filling me with awe and wonder. Amidst this captivating marine life, the curious gazes of New Zealand fur seals warmed my heart, reminding me of the beauty that lies in nature's simplest moments.

As I journeyed along the enchanting Abel Tasman Coast Track, I found solace in the native forests and revelled in the golden beaches that seemed to stretch to infinity. The harmonious melody of native birds served as my guide, and I felt a profound connection with the land that embraced me like an old friend.

But South Island's allure extended beyond its untamed beauty. I was embraced by warm hospitality and delectable seafood in the coastal towns, paired harmoniously with world-class wines that danced on my palate. The flavor of South Island's culinary delights became a symphony of taste, painting a vivid picture of the region's culture and charm.

"A First Time Visit" is more than a travelogue; it is a tale of wonder and self-discovery, narrated with passion and emotion. Allow my experiences to ignite your wanderlust and inspire you to uncover the enchanting secrets of South Island, New Zealand. This book beckons you to embark on your adventure, where every moment is an invitation to create memories that will forever reside in your heart. As you turn each page, you will be transported to a world of untamed beauty and alluring charm, forever cherishing the magic of "A First Time Visit" to South Island, New Zealand. Get ready to be captivated and inspired by this extraordinary journey that will leave you yearning for your own South Island escapade

Welcome to South Island, New Zealand

Welcome to the South Island, let's get started by displaying the map of this historic city and another centre of attractions.

Maps

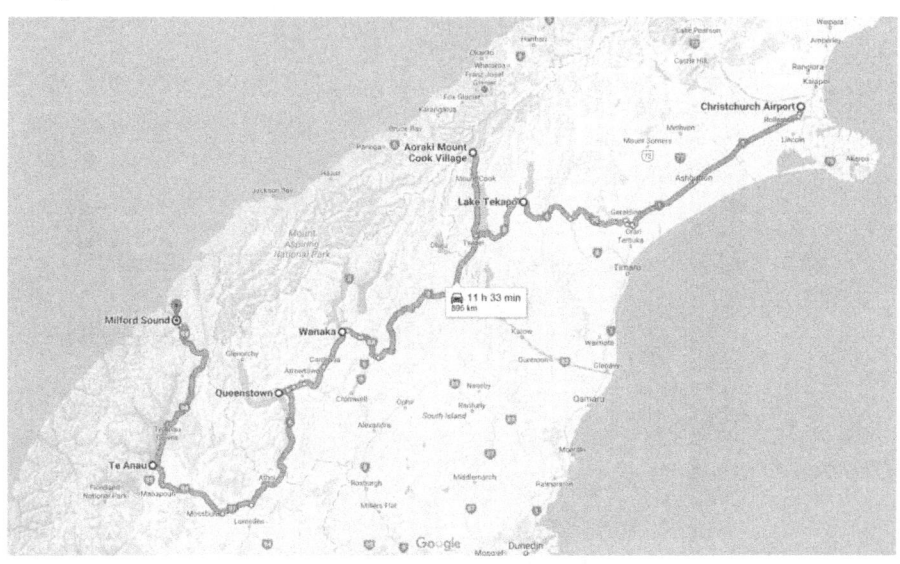

Source: *google map*

Centre of Attraction

Explained below are some of the top attractions in the South Island of New Zealand:

+ **Milford Sound**

    Milford Sound is a stunning fjord located in Fiordland National Park. Its name can be traced back to the early 19th century when John Grono, a sealer, named it after Milford Haven in Wales. The Maori name for Milford Sound is "Piopiotahi," which translates to "a single thrush," representing an extinct bird species found in the region. The awe-inspiring beauty of Milford Sound, with its towering cliffs and cascading waterfalls, has made it a popular tourist destination and a source of inspiration for poets and artists.

+ **Franz Josef Glacier**

The Franz Josef Glacier is a magnificent icy wonderland located in Westland Tai Poutini National Park. It was named after Emperor Franz Joseph I of Austria by Julius von Haast, a German geologist who explored the region in the 19th century. The glacier is known as "Kā Roimata o Hine Hukatere" in the Maori language, which translates to "The Tears of Hine Hukatere." According to Maori legend, Hine Hukatere was a young woman who lost her lover in an avalanche and her tears froze, forming the glacier.

+ **Abel Tasman National Park**

Abel Tasman National Park, named after the Dutch explorer Abel Tasman, is situated at the top of the South Island. Tasman was the first European to sight New Zealand in 1642. The park's Maori name is "Te Tai-o-Aorere," which translates to "The Tides of Aorere." The Aorere River flows through the park, and it holds cultural significance to the local Maori people, who have a rich history and connection to the area.

+ **Aoraki/Mount Cook National Park**

Aoraki/Mount Cook National Park is home to New Zealand's highest peak, Mount Cook. It was named after Captain James Cook, the British explorer who surveyed and mapped much of New Zealand's coastline during the late 18th century. The park's Maori name, Aoraki, means "cloud piercer" or "cloud in the sky." It holds great spiritual significance to the Ngāi

Tahu iwi (tribe), who consider Aoraki as an important ancestor and a sacred place.

+ **Lake Tekapo**

Lake Tekapo, known for its stunning turquoise-coloured waters, is located in the Mackenzie Basin. The name "Tekapo" has Māori origins, and its meaning is attributed to two possible explanations. One theory suggests that "Tekapo" means "tapping stone," referring to the practice of striking stones together to produce fire. Another theory suggests that it means "sleeping mat," as the shape of the lake resembles a traditional woven sleeping mat.

⊥ Queenstown

Queenstown, often referred to as the "Adventure Capital of the World," is a vibrant town nestled on the shores of Lake Wakatipu. It was named after Queen Victoria, the reigning British monarch during the time of the town's establishment in the 1800s. The Maori name for Queenstown is "Tāhuna," which translates to "shallow bay." The town's location and picturesque setting have contributed to its popularity as a tourist destination and a hub for adventure activities.

These attractions in the South Island of New Zealand not only showcase the natural beauty of the region but also hold historical and cultural significance, adding depth and meaning to their names. Exploring these attractions allows visitors to connect with the rich heritage and captivating stories that have shaped the South Island's identity.

New Zealand

CHAPTER ONE
History and Culture of South Island

The South Island of New Zealand boasts a captivating history and culture, shaped by the rich tapestry of Māori heritage, European settlement, and the diverse influences of Asian and Pacific Island communities. This island is a treasure trove of stories, traditions, and landmarks that reflect its unique identity and offer visitors an immersive experience of its fascinating past and vibrant present.

Pre-European Settlement

The pre-European settlement period in the South Island of New Zealand holds a captivating history that stretches back thousands of years. This era is characterized by the thriving indigenous Māori culture, where ancient traditions, customs, and knowledge were deeply rooted in the land. From the earliest Polynesian migrations to the establishment of thriving settlements, this period offers a window into the rich and diverse tapestry of Māori life before European arrival. Exploring the pre-European settlement of the South Island allows us to appreciate the deep connections between the indigenous people and the land, and to understand the foundations upon which the region's cultural heritage was built.

Polynesian Migrations and Early Settlement

The pre-European settlement period in the South Island begins with the Polynesian migrations when the ancestors of the Māori people first arrived in New Zealand around 800 CE. These early voyagers brought with them advanced seafaring skills and a rich oral tradition, which guided their journey across the vast Pacific Ocean. The South Island's rugged and untamed landscapes presented both challenges and opportunities for the early settlers.

Māori Culture and Traditions

The Māori established settlements along the South Island's coastlines, utilizing the bountiful resources provided by the surrounding land and sea. They relied on hunting, fishing, and gathering practices, adapting their lifestyle to the diverse environments of the region. The lush forests offered an abundance of timber for building homes, crafting canoes, and creating tools. The rivers and lakes provided sustenance through the cultivation of kumara (sweet potatoes), taro, and other crops.

Māori society was deeply connected to the natural world, and their cultural practices were intricately woven into their everyday lives. They embraced a holistic worldview that emphasized the interdependence of humans, nature, and the spiritual realm. Rituals and ceremonies were central to Māori life, honouring the land, ancestors, and gods.

Whakapapa (genealogy) played a vital role in Māori society, tracing lineage and establishing connections to the land. Oral traditions and storytelling preserved the histories, legends, and spiritual beliefs of the Māori people. These narratives were passed down through generations, shaping the cultural identity and collective memory of the communities.

Artistic expression also flourished during this period, with intricate carvings, woven textiles, and tattooing (moko) serving as important forms of cultural representation. The beauty and intricacy of Māori art reflected their deep reverence for the natural world and their ancestral connections.

Trade and intertribal relationships were fundamental aspects of Māori society in the pre-European settlement period. The South Island's unique geographical features, including its vast network of rivers and its abundance of resources, facilitated trade and communication between different tribal groups.

Pounamu, a type of jade or greenstone, held immense cultural significance for the Māori people. The South Island was home to significant pounamu deposits, and it became a highly sought-after resource for its beauty and spiritual significance. Tribes would travel long distances to the West Coast to access these precious stones, creating trade networks that spanned the country.

Trade routes also facilitated the exchange of knowledge, skills, and cultural practices between tribes. This intertribal exchange contributed to the richness and diversity of Māori culture, allowing different communities to learn from one another and adapt to new environments.

Archaeological Sites and Cultural Landmarks

The South Island is home to numerous archaeological sites that offer insights into the pre-European settlement period. These sites, such as Wairau Bar and Pyramid Valley, provide valuable evidence of early Māori settlement and the cultural practices of the time. Archaeologists have unearthed tools, artifacts, and remains that shed light on Māori life and the technological advancements of the period. Cultural landmarks, such as sacred mountains and lakes, hold deep spiritual and historical significance for the Māori people. Aoraki/Mount Cook, the tallest peak in New Zealand, is considered a sacred site and a link between the heavens and the earth. The beautiful Lake Pukaki, with its turquoise waters, is also of great cultural importance.

Early European Exploration and Colonization

The early European exploration and colonization of the South Island of New Zealand marked a significant chapter in its history, leaving an indelible impact on the region's culture, economy, and identity. This period, which began in the late 18th century, saw European explorers venturing into uncharted waters, followed by the establishment of settlements and the subsequent interactions between European settlers and the indigenous Māori population. This content explores the motivations behind European exploration, the process of colonization, and the resulting effects on the South Island's history and heritage.

European exploration of the South Island was driven by several motivations. The quest for new trade routes and resources, particularly in the lucrative Pacific region, fuelled the interest of European powers. Explorers sought to expand their empires, establish strategic outposts, and gain a competitive advantage in the global trade networks.

Scientific curiosity also played a role, as European explorers were eager to document and study the flora, fauna, and indigenous cultures of the lands they encountered. The South Island's unique geography and biodiversity provided fertile ground for scientific exploration, leading to important discoveries and contributions to the fields of botany, zoology, and anthropology.

European colonization of the South Island began with the arrival of Captain James Cook, who charted the coastlines of New Zealand during his voyages in the late 18th century. However, it was not until the early 19th century that significant European settlement took place.

European settlers were attracted to the South Island's fertile lands, abundant natural resources, and potential for agriculture and pastoralism. The establishment of permanent settlements, such as Christchurch, Dunedin, and Nelson, led to the rapid growth of European communities. These settlers brought with them their cultural practices, institutions, and technologies, shaping the social and economic landscape of the South Island. The arrival of European settlers had a profound impact on the indigenous Māori population. Initial encounters were often marked by curiosity and exchanges of goods, but as European settlement expanded, tensions arose over land ownership, cultural differences, and the introduction of new diseases.

The signing of the Treaty of Waitangi in 1840, which aimed to establish a partnership between Māori and the British Crown, had far-reaching implications for the relationship between European settlers and Māori communities. The interpretation and implementation of the treaty varied, leading to conflicts and land disputes that would shape the course of New Zealand's history.

The interactions between European settlers and Māori communities resulted in a complex process of cultural exchange, adaptation, and conflict. European settlers introduced new agricultural practices, technology, and institutions, while Māori communities shared their knowledge of the land, language, and cultural traditions.

However, conflicts over land ownership and cultural misunderstandings led to significant tensions. The New Zealand Wars of the 19th century, primarily fought in the North Island, had repercussions for the South Island as well, with Māori communities facing dispossession and displacement.

The European colonization of the South Island has left a lasting legacy on its history and heritage. European architecture, institutions, and place names are prevalent throughout the region, showcasing the influence of European settlement. The development of farming and agriculture, particularly sheep farming, shaped the economy and identity of the South Island, earning it the reputation of the "Sheep Farming Capital of the World."

However, efforts have been made to acknowledge and address the injustices faced by Māori communities during this period. The recognition of the Treaty of Waitangi as a founding document of New Zealand's nationhood, combined with ongoing treaty settlements, represents steps towards reconciliation and the revitalization of Māori culture and language.

Gold Rush and Development

The Gold Rushes of the 19th and early 20th centuries were transformative events that significantly influenced the development of regions and nations worldwide. The discovery of gold deposits ignited mass migrations, fostered economic growth, and spurred technological advancements. This comprehensive article delves into the history of the Gold Rush phenomena, their socio-economic implications, and their lasting impact on the development of affected areas.

+ The California Gold Rush, triggered by the discovery of gold at Sutter's Mill in 1848, drew hordes of fortune-seekers to the

American West. This event led to the rapid growth of California's population and laid the foundation for its future economic prominence.

- The discovery of gold in Australia (1850s-1860s), particularly in Victoria and New South Wales, fuelled massive waves of immigration, transforming the colonies into a significant economic force within the British Empire.

- The discovery of gold in the Klondike region of Yukon, Canada (1896-1899), triggered a frenzied rush of prospectors to the North, enhancing Canada's economic prospects and shaping its future development.

- The lure of gold-rich regions caused population explosions, as thousands of people from diverse backgrounds flocked to the goldfields in search of prosperity. This influx of people from different regions and countries accelerated cultural diversity and fostered multiculturalism in the affected areas.

- The demand for goods and services in gold rush regions led to the rapid development of infrastructure, including roads, railroads, ports, and communication networks. These developments laid the groundwork for further economic expansion beyond mining.

- Urbanization and Urban Development Gold rush settlements transformed into bustling towns and cities almost overnight. These urban centers became hubs for commerce, banking, and trade, thus shaping the socio-economic landscape of the regions for years to come.

- The pursuit of gold encouraged advancements in mining technology and techniques. Innovations such as hydraulic mining, steam-powered machinery, and more efficient extraction methods not only increased gold yields but also laid the groundwork for further industrialization.

- The rapid influx of people and the subsequent expansion of mining operations had significant environmental consequences. Deforestation, water pollution, and habitat destruction led to ecological imbalances, which still resonate in some gold rush regions today.

- The success of gold rush regions led to increased interest from the central government, which often resulted in territorial expansion and eventual statehood. This had profound political implications, shaping the balance of power within the nation.

- The Gold Rushes often occurred on lands traditionally inhabited by indigenous communities. The influx of miners and settlers disrupted their way of life, leading to conflicts over land rights and resources, resulting in significant political and social changes

* The gold rushes had lasting effects on the economies of the affected regions. Some areas continued to prosper due to diversification beyond mining, while others faced economic decline as gold reserves depleted.

* The Gold Rushes facilitated cultural exchange and migration patterns that continue to influence the demographic makeup of these regions to this day.

* The infrastructure and technological developments initiated during the Gold Rushes laid the foundation for long-term economic growth and industrialization in the affected regions.

* Environmental Conservation Efforts In light of the environmental damage caused by mining activities during the Gold Rushes, subsequent conservation efforts have emerged, focusing on preserving and restoring the ecosystems affected by gold mining.

Modern South Island

The modern history of the South Island of New Zealand is a captivating tale of development, cultural diversity, and environmental preservation. This overview concentrates on the significant events and transformations that have shaped the region in the 20th and 21st centuries, showcasing the South Island's emergence as a prominent tourist destination, its commitment to conservation, and the challenges it faces in the modern era.

1. **Tourism and Recreation:**

    a. **Emergence as a Tourist Destination:** The South Island has witnessed a remarkable surge in tourism, attracting visitors from all corners of the globe. Its pristine landscapes, including the Southern Alps, Fiordland National Park, and the Marlborough Sounds, have made it a haven for adventure seekers, nature enthusiasts, and those seeking tranquillity.

    b. **Adventure Tourism**: The South Island has become renowned for its adrenaline-fueled adventure activities such as bungee jumping, skydiving, jet boating, and heli-skiing. These activities have contributed significantly to the region's economy and have made it a global hub for thrill-seekers.

    c. **Ecotourism and Nature Conservation:** The South Island's commitment to preserving its natural wonders has resulted in the development of ecotourism initiatives. Protected areas, such as Abel Tasman National Park and the Catlins, offer opportunities for visitors to experience untouched beauty while promoting sustainable practices and environmental education.

2. Environmental Conservation:

   a. **National Parks and World Heritage Sites:** The South Island is home to several national parks and UNESCO World Heritage Sites. These include Fiordland National Park, Mount Aspiring National Park, Aoraki/Mount Cook National Park, and Te Wahipounamu (South West New Zealand) World Heritage Area. These protected areas preserve unique ecosystems, endangered species, and breathtaking landscapes.

   b. **Biodiversity Protection:** Conservation efforts on the South Island have focused on preserving endemic species, including the rare and flightless kiwi bird. Various sanctuaries and predator-free islands, such as

Ulva Island and Tiritiri Matangi Island, have been established to protect native flora and fauna.

3. Economic Development:

   a. **Agriculture and Viticulture:** The South Island's fertile land supports a thriving agricultural industry, with sheep farming, dairy farming, and viticulture being key contributors to the economy. The region produces high-quality wines, particularly in the Marlborough and Central Otago wine-growing regions.

   b. **Film and Creative Industries:** The South Island has served as a backdrop for numerous international film productions, most notably the "The Lord of the Rings" and "The Hobbit" trilogies. This has led to the growth of the creative industries, including film production, visual effects, and tourism-related services.

4. Infrastructure and Connectivity:

   a. **Transport Networks:** The South Island has witnessed significant developments in its transport infrastructure. Improved highways, such as State

Highway 1 and State Highway 6, have enhanced connectivity between towns and cities. Additionally, the South Island boasts world-class airports, facilitating domestic and international travel.

b. **Digital Connectivity:** The proliferation of high-speed internet and telecommunications services has connected the South Island to the global digital network, enabling businesses, communities, and individuals to participate in the modern digital economy.

5. **Cultural Diversity:**

a. **Māori Cultural Revival:** The South Island has experienced a resurgence in Māori cultural pride and identity. Māori language revitalization efforts, cultural festivals, and the establishment of cultural centers have helped preserve and celebrate Māori heritage and traditions.

b. **Multiculturalism:** The South Island's communities have become increasingly diverse due to immigration from various countries. This multiculturalism has enriched the region's cultural fabric, fostered cross-cultural understanding, and contributed to vibrant local communities.

6. **Environmental Challenges:**

   a. **Climate Change Mitigation:** The South Island, like the rest of the world, faces the challenges of climate change. Efforts are underway to reduce greenhouse gas emissions, promote renewable energy sources, and adapt to changing environmental conditions.

   b. **Conservation and Sustainability:** The South Island continues to grapple with the delicate balance between tourism development and environmental preservation. Ensuring sustainable practices, minimizing ecological impact, and protecting sensitive areas remain ongoing challenges.

Heritage

The South Island of New Zealand is not only renowned for its breath-taking landscapes but also boasts a rich and diverse legacy. From ancient Māori settlements to the era of European colonization, the heritage of South Island narrates a captivating tale of cultural traditions, historical events, and the amalgamation of diverse communities. This article delves into the legacy of contemporary South Island, exploring its Māori inheritance, European influence, and the conservation of cultural landmarks.

a. Māori Inheritance:

The Māori people possess a profound affinity with the land and sea of South Island, which they call Te Waipounamu. Their history is deeply ingrained in the topography through sacred sites, archaeological remnants, and ancestral narratives passed down through generations. South Island is home to several notable Māori settlements, including Kaiapoi, Ōnawe, and Wairau Bar, which offer valuable insights into the region's culturally affluent heritage.

b. European Colonization:

The commencement of European exploration and colonization on South Island can be traced back to the arrival of Captain James Cook in the late 18th century. The subsequent influx of European settlers left an indelible mark on the region's heritage. Towns such as Christchurch, Dunedin, and Nelson serve as testaments to European influence, characterized by their distinct architectural styles, institutional establishments, and historical landmarks. Moreover, the impact of European settlers is evident in agricultural practices, infrastructure development, and the introduction of novel industries.

c. Cultural Landmarks:

South Island is adorned with cultural landmarks that serve as poignant reminders of its heritage. For instance, the Otago Peninsula houses historical sites like Larnach Castle, an impressive testament to the region's colonial past. In Christchurch, the Canterbury Museum houses an extensive collection of artifacts and exhibitions that shed light on both Māori and European heritage. Likewise, the Otago Settlers Museum in Dunedin offers a glimpse into the lives of early European settlers and their profound influence on the region.

d. Conservation Endeavours:

Recognizing the significance of South Island's heritage, earnest efforts have been made to conserve and safeguard cultural landmarks. Organizations such as Heritage New Zealand tirelessly work towards protecting historic sites and ensuring public access to these invaluable treasures. The collaborative efforts between Māori communities, local authorities, and heritage organizations have played a pivotal role in preserving Māori heritage and fostering cultural understanding.

e. **Cultural Festivals and Events:**

South Island proudly hosts a diverse range of cultural festivals and events that celebrate its rich heritage. The Hokitika Wildfoods Festival showcases the region's distinctive culinary traditions, while the Nelson Arts Festival shines a spotlight on local arts and crafts. Furthermore, the annual Waitangi Day commemorations provide a significant platform to honor the signing of New Zealand's founding document and celebrate the vibrant Māori culture.

CHAPTER TWO

Travel Planning Essentials

Prepare for an extraordinary journey to the captivating South Island of New Zealand with our essential travel guide, we've got you covered. Unveil the necessary travel essentials and embark on an unforgettable exploration of this breath-taking paradise.

Visa and Entry Requirements

Visa and entry requirements to the South Island of New Zealand vary for indigenous New Zealanders and foreign nationals. For indigenous New Zealanders, who hold New Zealand citizenship or a valid New Zealand passport, there are no visa requirements. They have the freedom to enter and explore the South Island without any restrictions.

On the other hand, for individuals from different countries, a visa is generally required to enter New Zealand, including the South Island. Here are the steps involved in obtaining a visa for visiting the South Island:

1. Determine the visa type:

   Identify the appropriate visa category based on the purpose of your visit, such as a tourist visa, work visa, student visa, or other relevant categories. Visit the official website of Immigration New Zealand (www.immigration.govt.nz) to explore the different visa options and their requirements.

2. Check eligibility:

Review the eligibility criteria and ensure that you meet the specific requirements for the chosen visa category. Factors like age, health, character, and financial capacity may be taken into consideration.

3. Gather required documents:

Prepare all the necessary documents, which may include a valid passport, proof of funds, travel itinerary, accommodation details, health insurance, and any other documents specific to your visa type. Ensure that your passport is valid for at least six months beyond your intended departure date.

4. Submit visa application:

Complete the visa application form accurately and submit it along with the required supporting documents to the nearest New Zealand embassy, consulate, or visa application center in your home country. Some visa applications can also be submitted online through the Immigration New Zealand website.

5. **Pay the visa fees:**

Pay the applicable visa fees, which may vary depending on the visa type and your nationality. The payment can be made online or as per the instructions provided by the visa application center.

6. **Attend any necessary appointments:**

Depending on the visa category, you may be required to attend an interview or provide biometric information (such as fingerprints and photographs) at a designated visa application center.

7. **Wait for processing:**

After submitting your application, wait for the visa processing time, which can vary based on the visa type and the number of applications being processed. Check the official website for estimated processing times.

8. **Receive the visa decision:**

Once the visa application is processed, you will receive a decision regarding your visa. If approved, your passport will be stamped with the visa or you will receive an electronic visa.

It is essential to apply for the visa well in advance of your intended travel dates to allow sufficient processing time. It is also recommended to consult the official website of Immigration New Zealand or contact the nearest New Zealand embassy or consulate for the most up-to-date and accurate information regarding visa requirements and procedures.

Customs and Immigration Procedures

When traveling to the South Island of New Zealand, it's important to be aware of the customs and immigration procedures to ensure a smooth entry into the country. Here are some key points to keep in mind:

1. Customs Procedures:

- **Declare goods:** Upon arrival, you will need to complete a Passenger Arrival Card. Be honest and declare any items that are restricted or require payment of duty, such as certain food products, animal products, plants, firearms, or large sums of cash.

- **Biosecurity checks:** New Zealand has strict biosecurity regulations to protect its unique environment. Ensure that your belongings are free from any biosecurity risk, such as soil, plants, or outdoor equipment. Declare any outdoor gear, hiking boots, or camping equipment for inspection.

- **Prohibited items:** Familiarize yourself with the list of prohibited items, including illicit drugs, weapons, and protected wildlife products. Attempting to bring these items into the country can result in severe penalties.

2. **Immigration Procedures:**

- **Valid passport:** Ensure that your passport is valid for at least three months beyond your intended departure date from New Zealand.

- **Visa requirements:** Check whether you require a visa to enter New Zealand based on your nationality and purpose of visit. Apply for the appropriate visa well in advance of your travel dates.

- **Electronic Travel Authority (ETA):** Some nationalities are required to obtain an ETA before traveling to New Zealand. Visit the official website of Immigration New Zealand to check if this applies to you.

- **Passenger Arrival Card:** Complete the Passenger Arrival Card with accurate information regarding your purpose of visit, duration of stay, and intended address in New Zealand.

3. Arrival and Customs Screening:

- **Quarantine procedures:** Prepare to undergo health screenings and answer questions related to your health and recent travel history, especially in response to global health concerns.

- **Customs inspection:** After collecting your luggage, proceed through the customs area where your belongings may be subject to random inspections. Follow the instructions of customs officers and declare any items as required.

It's important to comply with all customs and immigration procedures to ensure a positive travel experience. Be patient, respectful, and cooperative throughout the process. For the most up-to-date and detailed information, visit the official websites of the New Zealand Customs Service and Immigration New Zealand or consult with the nearest New Zealand embassy or consulate in your home country.

Health and Safety Tips

When exploring the stunning South Island of New Zealand, it's essential to prioritize your health and safety. Here are some compelling tips to ensure a well-structured and enjoyable journey:

1. **Prepare Adequate Travel Insurance:**

   - Prioritize travel insurance that covers medical emergencies, trip cancellations, and personal belongings.

   - Ensure your insurance policy includes outdoor activities, such as hiking, skiing, and water sports.

2. **Stay Hydrated and Protected from the Sun:**

   - Carry a reusable water bottle and stay hydrated, especially during outdoor activities.

   - Apply sunscreen with a high SPF, wear sunglasses, and a wide-brimmed hat to protect against New Zealand's strong UV rays.

3. **Dress Appropriately for the Weather and Terrain:**

   - Layer clothing to adapt to New Zealand's changeable weather conditions.

- Wear sturdy footwear for hiking and exploring uneven terrains.

4. **Adhere to Outdoor Safety Guidelines:**

- Check weather forecasts and be prepared for sudden weather changes.

- Inform someone of your hiking or outdoor activity plans, including expected return time.

- Carry a map, compass, and a reliable means of communication, such as a fully charged mobile phone or a personal locator beacon.

5. **Respect Nature and Wildlife:**

- Follow designated tracks and trails to minimize environmental impact.

- Keep a safe distance from wildlife, and never feed or disturb them.

6. **Take Precautions in the Outdoors:**

- Be cautious of unstable terrain, fast-flowing rivers, and sudden changes in water depth.

- Take note of safety signs and follow instructions at beaches and other natural attractions.

7. **Be Mindful of Driving Safety:**

- Follow New Zealand's Road rules and drive on the left-hand side of the road.

- Take breaks during long drives, and avoid driving under the influence of alcohol or fatigue.

8. **Prioritize Personal Well-being:**

- Get sufficient rest and manage your energy levels during your journey.

- Maintain a balanced diet and carry healthy snacks for outdoor activities.

- Seek medical attention if you experience any health concerns or injuries.

Remember, your health and safety are paramount during your South Island adventure. By adhering to these tips and staying informed, you can fully immerse yourself in the breathtaking landscapes and experiences that the South Island has to offer. Enjoy your journey responsibly, and always prioritize your well-being.

Travel Insurance

Travel insurance is an essential component of any trip, providing protection and peace of mind throughout your travels. It offers financial coverage for unforeseen events, medical emergencies, trip cancellations, and lost or stolen belongings. Here's a breakdown of the essence of travel insurance and how to obtain it:

1. Coverage for Medical Emergencies:

    - Travel insurance ensures access to medical treatment in case of unexpected illnesses or injuries while traveling.

    - It may cover medical expenses, hospitalization, emergency medical evacuation, and repatriation.

2. Protection for Trip Cancellations or Delays:

    - Travel insurance safeguards your investment by reimbursing non-refundable trip costs in case of trip cancellations, interruptions, or delays due to covered reasons, such as illness, natural disasters, or airline strikes.

    - It can also provide reimbursement for additional expenses incurred during these situations.

3. **Lost or Stolen Belongings:**

- Travel insurance covers the loss, theft, or damage of personal belongings, including luggage, travel documents, and valuables.

- It provides compensation for the replacement of essential items to minimize disruption to your trip.

4. **Assistance Services:**

- Travel insurance often includes 24/7 emergency assistance services to help you navigate unexpected situations, such as medical emergencies, lost passports, or travel disruptions.

- These services provide access to multilingual support, emergency cash transfers, and travel advice.

Steps for obtaining Travel Insurance:

1. Research and Compare Plans:

- Research different travel insurance providers and compare their coverage, benefits, exclusions, and prices.

- Consider the specific needs of your trip, such as destination, duration, activities, and any pre-existing medical conditions.

2. **Determine the Coverage You Need:**

- Assess the level of coverage required for medical expenses, trip cancellation/interruption, baggage loss, and other aspects based on your travel plans.

- Ensure that the insurance policy covers the destinations you intend to visit and any high-risk activities you may participate in, such as adventure sports.

3. **Purchase the Policy:**

- Once you have chosen a suitable travel insurance plan, visit the insurer's website or contact their customer service to purchase the policy.

- Provide the necessary information, including your travel dates, destination, personal details, and payment information.

4. **Review the Policy Terms and Conditions:**

- Carefully read through the policy documentation, including the terms and conditions, coverage limits, deductibles, and any exclusions.

- Understand the claims process and the required documentation in case you need to file a claim.

5. **Carry Proof of Insurance:**

- Print a copy of your travel insurance policy or have an electronic version readily accessible during your trip.

- Keep the emergency contact details of your insurer and your policy number handy.

Currency and Banking Information

Understanding currency and banking information is crucial when traveling to a new country. Here is a comprehensive guide to currency exchange, banking services, and financial tips for your trip:

1. **Currency Exchange:**

   - The official currency of New Zealand is the New Zealand Dollar (NZD). Familiarize yourself with the current exchange rate before your trip.

   - Exchange currency at authorized outlets such as banks, currency exchange offices, or ATMs for competitive rates. Avoid exchanging money at airports or unauthorized street vendors, as they often charge higher fees.

   - Carry a mix of cash and cards for convenience and emergencies. Major credit and debit cards are widely accepted in most establishments.

2. **Banking Services:**

   - Banks in New Zealand typically operate from Monday to Friday, with some branches open on Saturdays. Business hours may vary, so check with individual banks for specific times.

- ATMs are widely available throughout the country, allowing you to withdraw cash using your debit or credit card. Be aware that fees may apply, so check with your home bank regarding any international transaction charges.

- Inform your bank about your travel plans to avoid your card being blocked due to suspected fraud. Inquire about any foreign transaction fees or withdrawal limits imposed by your bank.

3. **Payment Options:**

- **Cash:** Carry a sufficient amount of New Zealand Dollars for small purchases, markets, and places that may not accept cards. Keep cash secure and be mindful of pickpockets.

- **Credit and Debit Cards:** Most businesses, including hotels, restaurants, and retail stores, accept major credit cards like Visa and Mastercard. Debit cards with a Visa or Mastercard logo can be used for purchases and cash withdrawals at ATMs.

- **Contactless Payments:** New Zealand widely accepts contactless payment methods like Apple Pay, Google Pay, and other mobile wallet services.

4. Safety and Security:

- Use secure ATMs located within banks or well-lit areas. Avoid ATMs in secluded or poorly monitored locations.

- Keep your PINs and personal information confidential. Shield your PIN when entering it at ATMs or point-of-sale terminals.

- Safeguard your cards and money by using a money belt or a secure wallet. Split your cash and cards between different pockets or bags for added security.

5. Budgeting and Expenses:

- Plan your budget in advance by considering accommodation, meals, transportation, activities, and any additional expenses.

- Research and compare prices to estimate daily costs and allocate funds accordingly.

- Consider unforeseen expenses, such as medical emergencies or changes in travel plans, and factor in travel insurance to provide financial protection.

6. Taxes and Tips:

- Goods and Services Tax (GST) of 15% is included in the price of most goods and services in New Zealand.

- Tipping is not customary in New Zealand, as service charges are generally included in the bill. However, leaving a small tip for exceptional service is appreciated but not obligatory.

Communication and Internet Services

Communication and internet services are vital for staying connected and accessing information while traveling. Here is a comprehensive guide to communication options, internet services, and network availability:

1. Mobile Networks and SIM Cards:

- New Zealand has reliable mobile networks, including Spark, Vodafone, and 2degrees, offering extensive coverage across the country.

- If your mobile device is unlocked, you can purchase a local prepaid SIM card upon arrival. SIM cards are available at airports, convenience stores, and mobile network provider outlets.

- Prepaid SIM cards offer data, calling, and messaging services at competitive rates, allowing you to stay connected with friends, and family, and access the internet.

2. Wi-Fi Availability:

- Wi-Fi is widely available in cafes, restaurants, hotels, libraries, and other public places throughout New Zealand. Most accommodations offer free or paid Wi-Fi access for guests.

- Public libraries often provide free Wi-Fi, and some cities have free Wi-Fi hotspots in popular tourist areas.

3. Internet Services and Cybercafés:

- Internet cafes or cybercafés are less common in New Zealand, but major cities still have a few establishments offering computer and internet access for a fee.

- If you don't have a mobile device or require more extensive internet access, consider visiting libraries, co-working spaces, or dedicated internet centres.

4. **Communication Apps and Services:**

- Utilize communication apps like WhatsApp, Skype, FaceTime, or Facebook Messenger to make voice and video calls over Wi-Fi or mobile data.

- These apps are convenient and cost-effective alternatives to traditional phone calls or SMS when communicating with friends and family internationally.

5. **Emergency Services:**

- In case of emergencies, dial 111 for immediate assistance in New Zealand. This number connects you to police, ambulance, or fire services.

- It is recommended to have local emergency contacts saved in your phone or written down for quick access.

6. **Roaming and International Calls:**

- Check with your mobile service provider about international roaming options and charges before your trip. Roaming may incur additional fees, so it's important to understand the costs and data limits.

- To make international calls, consider using Voice over Internet Protocol (VoIP) services like Skype or purchasing a calling card for cost-effective options.

7. **Network Availability in Remote Areas:**

- While urban and popular tourist areas have excellent network coverage, remote or mountainous regions may have limited or no mobile reception.

- If you plan to venture into remote areas, inform someone of your plans, carry a map or GPS device, and consider investing in a personal locator beacon for emergencies.

CHAPTER THREE

South Island Overview

Embark on a captivating journey through the alluring charm of New Zealand's South Island, where the supremacy of nature and the promise of adventure converge at every twist and turn. Immerse yourself in a realm of awe-inspiring landscapes, unspoiled wilderness, and exhilarating escapades that will leave you in a state of breathless wonder.

Prepare to be enchanted by the majestic Southern Alps, an imposing mountain range that spans the entirety of the island, bestowing unparalleled magnificence and infinite possibilities for outdoor exploration. From the snow-dusted summits to the glacier-carved valleys and pristine alpine lakes, the panoramic vistas here will cast a spell upon your senses.

Embark on a journey through Fiordland National Park, a hallowed sanctuary recognized as a UNESCO World Heritage Site, and bear witness to the sheer grandeur of its awe-inspiring fiords. Milford Sound and Doubtful Sound will transfix you with their dramatic cliffs and cascading waterfalls, as you embark on a voyage through these natural wonders, forging cherished memories that will endure throughout a lifetime.

For those who seek the thrill of adrenaline, Queenstown stands as an unrivaled playground. Brace yourself for heart-pounding activities such as bungee jumping, jet boating, and skydiving, all against the backdrop of breath-taking mountain vistas. And when winter blankets the region, the Remarkable transform into a haven for skiers, offering exhilarating slopes and unparalleled alpine experiences.

Enthusiasts of nature will find solace in the embrace of Abel Tasman National Park, where golden beaches, crystalline waters, and lush forests await. Traverse the Abel Tasman Coast Track on foot or paddle along the tranquil bays in a kayak, encountering indigenous wildlife and luxuriating in the tranquillity of this coastal paradise.

The untamed West Coast beckons with its unexplored paths and rugged beauty. Venture into the depths of Franz Josef Glacier and Fox Glacier, marveling at their icy azure tones and experiencing the exhilaration of treading upon ancient ice. Unspoiled rainforests and secluded beaches further enhance the allure of this remote region, evoking a sense of exploration and awe-inspiring fascination.

Indulge in the flavours of Marlborough, a renowned region celebrated for its world-class wines, particularly the crisp and vivacious Sauvignon Blanc. Relish the delicate aromas and savour the fruits of the vineyards as you immerse yourself in the breath-taking vistas of undulating hills and sun-kissed landscapes.

While traversing the South Island, vibrant cities will captivate you with their distinctive allure. Christchurch, with its rejuvenated city center and flourishing arts scene, extends a warm invitation to explore its botanical gardens and embrace its gracious hospitality. Dunedin, renowned for its Scottish heritage and remarkable wildlife, beckons you to admire its historic architecture and encounter the majestic royal albatross.

The South Island of New Zealand is a realm where dreams take flight, where nature paints its most vivid masterpiece, and where the spirit of adventure weaves itself into the fabric of everyday life. Immerse yourself in the magic and wonder of this extraordinary island, and allow its unparalleled beauty to leave an indelible imprint upon the very depths of your soul.

Geography and Climate

South Island is the larger of New Zealand's two main islands, boasting a land area of around 150,000 square kilometers. Its geography is characterized by remarkable contrasts, from snow-capped mountains to pristine lakes, dense forests, and rugged coastlines. The island is divided by the awe-inspiring Southern Alps, a mountain range that stretches for over 500 kilometers. Mount Cook, New Zealand's highest peak, proudly stands amidst this majestic range.

Fiordland, located in the southwest, showcases some of South Island's most mesmerizing natural wonders. Milford Sound, Doubtful Sound, and Dusky Sound, with their towering cliffs and cascading waterfalls, beckon adventurers to immerse themselves in their grandeur. These fiords are the result of glacial erosion over thousands of years, leaving behind a landscape that is both dramatic and awe-inspiring.

The Canterbury Plains dominate the eastern side of the island, providing a stark contrast to the mountainous regions. This vast expanse of flat land, bordered by the Southern Alps and the Pacific Ocean, is home to lush farmlands, vibrant vineyards, and charming coastal towns.

The West Coast is a rugged and untamed region, where dense rainforests meet the wild Tasman Sea. Its remarkable landscapes include the Fox and Franz Josef glaciers, which descend from the Southern Alps into lush rainforests an incredibly rare sight indeed.

Wild Tasman Sea

South Island's climate is influenced by its diverse topography, with significant variations from region to region. The west coast experiences a temperate maritime climate, characterized by high rainfall and mild temperatures throughout the year. Here, lush rainforests thrive, creating a haven for unique flora and fauna. Be prepared for sudden weather changes, as the mountains often trap moisture-laden clouds, leading to frequent rain showers.

As you venture eastward, the climate becomes drier, with the Canterbury Plains experiencing a temperate climate. Summers are warm and dry, perfect for exploring the vibrant city of Christchurch and indulging in outdoor activities such as hiking, cycling, and wine tasting.

In the mountainous regions, including the Southern Alps, the climate transitions to an alpine climate. The weather here is characterized by cooler temperatures, especially at higher elevations, and snowfall during the winter months. These majestic peaks offer thrilling opportunities for mountaineering, skiing, and snowboarding.

For those seeking an extraordinary experience, the Central Otago region offers a unique semi-continental climate. With scorching hot summers and bitterly cold winters, this region produces world-class wines, thanks to the special combination of climate and unique soils.

Whether you're an adventurer or a student of geography, South Island's geography and climate provide an endless array of opportunities for exploration and learning. From scaling towering peaks to cruising through mesmerizing fiords, studying glacial formations, or immersing yourself in diverse ecosystems, the wonders of South Island will leave an indelible mark on your soul.

Wildlife and Natural Features

South Island, located in New Zealand, is a captivating destination renowned for its stunning natural beauty. This enchanting landmass boasts an incredible array of wildlife and natural features that make it a paradise for nature lovers and adventurers. From majestic mountains to pristine lakes, and lush forests to diverse ecosystems, South Island is a treasure trove waiting to be explored. In this article, we will delve into mesmerizing wildlife and explore the fascinating history of some of the key natural features found on this remarkable island.

Wildlife:

1. **Kiwi Bird (*Apteryx*):**

   The Kiwi bird, a national symbol of New Zealand, is a flightless bird endemic to the country. Several species of Kiwi can be found on South Island, each with unique physical and anatomical features. These small, stocky birds possess hair-like feathers, which resemble coarse fur. They have long, slender bills perfect for probing the forest floor in search of insects, worms, and grubs. Kiwis also possess strong legs and muscular thighs, enabling them to move swiftly through the underbrush.

2. **Hector's Dolphin (*Cephalorhynchus hectori*):**

Hector's Dolphin is one of the world's smallest and rarest dolphin species, and it calls the waters around South Island home. These delightful creatures feature a rounded dorsal fin and a short, stocky body. They have distinctive black, white, and gray markings, giving them a striking appearance. Hector's Dolphins are highly social and often display playful behavior, making encounters with them an unforgettable experience.

3. **Kea (*Nestor notabilis*):**

The Kea is an intelligent and mischievous parrot species found in the alpine regions of South Island. Renowned for its curiosity and sociability, the Kea has a vibrant plumage with shades of green and blue. It possesses a powerful beak designed for eating a wide variety of food, including plant matter, insects, and even carrion. Keas are known for their playful nature, often engaging in aerial acrobatics and entertaining antics.

4. Fiordland Crested Penguin (*Eudyptes pachyrhynchus*):

The Fiordland Crested Penguin, also known as the Tawaki, is a unique penguin species that breed in the dense rainforests of South Island's west coast. This penguin boasts distinct yellow crests above its eyes, giving it a regal appearance. Its body is covered in waterproof feathers, enabling it to swim effortlessly in the frigid waters. The Fiordland Crested Penguin's strong flippers and streamlined body make it an excellent swimmer and diver.

5. New Zealand Fur Seal (*Arctocephalus forsteri*):

The New Zealand Fur Seal, or Kekeno, is a charismatic marine mammal found along the coastlines of the South Island. With a sleek and streamlined body, these seals are well-adapted for life in the ocean. They possess long, sensitive whiskers, called vibrissae, which aid in detecting prey underwater. New Zealand Fur Seals have flippers that enable them to maneuver swiftly through the water and a thick fur coat to keep them warm in cooler climates.

6. Yellow-eyed Penguin (*Megadyptes antipodes*):

The Yellow-eyed Penguin, also known as Hoiho, is a rare and endangered species native to New Zealand. It has distinct yellow eyes, a yellow band across its head, and a unique yellow crest. These penguins have slender nobodies and zipper-likings that enable them to swim swiftly through the water in search of small fish and squid.

7. Saddleback (*Philesturnus carunculatus*):

The Saddleback, or Tieke, is a medium-sized bird endemic to New Zealand. It has a distinctive black head with a vibrant chestnut-colored saddle-like patch on its back. Saddlebacks possess a strong beak adapted for feeding on insects, spiders, and nectar. They are known for their melodious songs and are a symbol of forest restoration success.

8. **South Island Kōkako (*Callaeas cinereus*):** The South Island Kōkako is a rare and elusive bird species with bluish-gray plumage and a striking blue wattle. It has a melodious and haunting song that echoes through the native forests. Although sightings are rare, efforts are being made to protect and conserve this species and its habitat.

9. New Zealand Falcon (*Falco novaeseelandiae*):

The New Zealand Falcon, or Kārearea, is a powerful bird of prey found throughout the South Island. It has a compact body, sharp talons, and a hooked beak ideal for capturing and feeding small birds and mammals. With incredible speed and agility, the New Zealand Falcon is a skilled hunter and a symbol of strength and resilience.

10. **South Island Robin (*Petroica australis*):**

The South Island Robin, or Toutouwai, is a small, friendly bird endemic to South Island's forests. It has a dark gray back, a white belly, and a distinct patch of bright orange-red on its breast. South Island Robins are known for their inquisitive nature, often following hikers along forest trails in search of insects and small invertebrates.

11. New Zealand Rock Wren (*Xenicus gilviventris*):

The New Zealand Rock Wren, or Piwauwau, is a unique and agile bird that thrives in alpine environments. It has mottled brown plumage and a long, downward-curving beak perfect for extracting insects from rock crevices. This wren is known for its ability to navigate cliffs and boulder fields with ease.

12. Stewart Island Brown Kiwi (*Apteryx australis*):

The Stewart Island Brown Kiwi, or Tokoeka, is a subspecies of the iconic Kiwi bird found on Stewart Island and surrounding islets. It has coarse, shaggy brown feathers and a long, curved beak for probing the forest floor in search of insects and worms. The Stewart Island Brown Kiwi is primarily nocturnal and has a distinctive, haunting call.

13. Kākāpō (*Strigops habroptila*):

The Kākāpō is a critically endangered parrot species and one of the world's rarest birds. It is a flightless and nocturnal bird with mossy green feathers that provide excellent camouflage in its native forest habitat. Kākāpō is known for its unusual breeding behavior and distinctive booming call.

14. South Island Takahe (*Porphyrio hochstetteri*):

The South Island Takahe is a large, flightless bird with vibrant blue and green feathers, a red beak, and long legs. Once thought to be extinct, this species was rediscovered in the Murchison Mountains of South Island. The South Island Takahe is a symbol of conservation success and is now protected in special reserves.

15. Southern Right Whale *(Eubalaena australis)*:

The Southern Right Whale is a magnificent marine mammal that visits the coastal waters of the South Island during winter and spring. They have a massive, robust body and lack a dorsal fin. These whales are known for their playful behaviour, breaching, and slapping their tails on the water's surface.

16. New Zealand Sea Lion (*Phocarctos hookeri*):

The New Zealand Sea Lion, or Whakahao, is one of the rarest sea lion species in the world. It has a large, barrel-shaped body, a short snout, and distinctive lion-like manes on the males. These sea lions breed on South Island's sandy beaches and rocky shores, and their populations are carefully monitored and protected.

17. Little Blue Penguin (*Eudyptula minor*):

The Little Blue Penguin, also known as the Kororā, is the world's smallest penguin species. It has slate-blue feathers and a white belly. These penguins spend their days at sea, returning to the coast at dusk to nest in burrows or under vegetation. Little Blue Penguins are excellent swimmers and put on delightful displays as they waddle ashore.

18. Yellow-crowned Parakeet (*Cyanoramphus triceps*):

The Yellow-crowned Parakeet, or Mohua, is a small and colorful bird endemic to South Island. It has a bright yellow crown, a green body, and a red beak. These parakeets inhabit native forests and are highly threatened due to habitat loss and predation. Conservation efforts are underway to protect this vulnerable species.

19. Australasian Gannet *(Morus serrator):*

The Australasian Gannet is a seabird that breeds in colonies on coastal cliffs and islands around South Island. It has striking white plumage with black wingtips and a distinctive golden head. Australasian Gannets are remarkable divers, plunging into the ocean at high speeds to catch fish.

20. New Zealand Pipit *(Anthus novaeseelandiae):*

The New Zealand Pipit, or Pīhoihoi, is a small bird found in grasslands, coastal dunes, and alpine meadows of the South Island. It's streaked brown plumage, a long tail, and a slender bill. These pipits are known for their distinctive display flight, accompanied by a delightful song.

21. Long-tailed Bat (*Chalinolobus tuberculatus*):

The Long-tailed Bat, or Pekepeke, is a small native bat species found in the forests and wetlands of South Island. It has brown fur, long wings, and a long tail. Long-tailed Bats are nocturnal and play a vital role in pollination and seed dispersal.

22. Giant Wētā (*Deinacrida spp.*):

The Giant Wētā is a group of large, flightless insects found in the forests of South Island. They are among the world's heaviest insects, with some species reaching over 8 cm (3 inches) in length. Giant Wētā has robust bodies, strong mandibles, and powerful hind legs for defense and jumping.

23. Southern Alps Gecko (*Woodworthia spp.*):

The Southern Alps Gecko is a unique lizard species endemic to the Southern Alps of South Island. It has a slender body, large eyes, and a distinctive pattern of light and dark markings. These geckos are well-adapted to alpine environments and are active at night, hunting for insects and other small invertebrates.

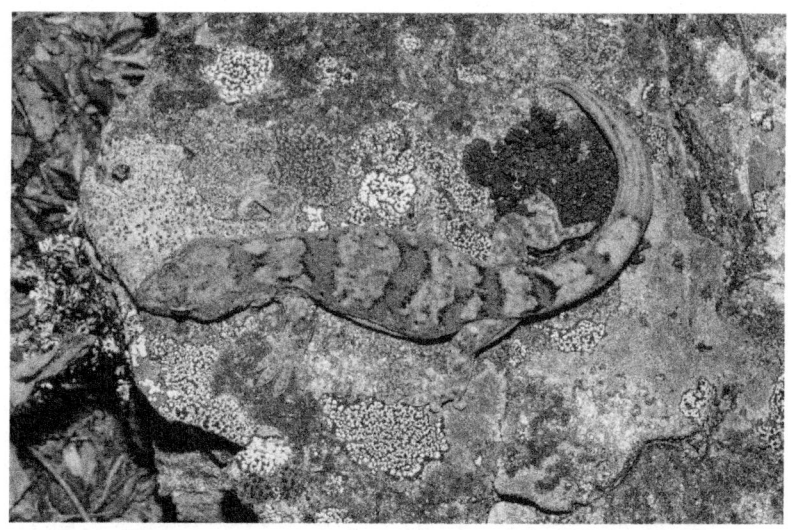

24. Marlborough Green Gecko (*Naultinus manukanus*):

The Marlborough Green Gecko is a stunning lizard species found in the Marlborough region of South Island. It has bright green skin with distinctive patterns and large, expressive eyes. These geckos are arboreal, spending most of their time in trees and shrubs.

25. Giant Kokopu (*Galaxius argenteus*):

The Giant Kokopu is a large native fish species found in rivers and streams throughout South Island. It has a sleek, silvery body and can grow up to 50 cm (20 inches) in length. These fish are nocturnal and are an important part of the freshwater ecosystem.

26. Giant Bull Kelp (*Durvillaea spp.*):

The Giant Bull Kelp is a species of seaweed found in the coastal waters around South Island. It has long, leathery fronds that can reach several meters in length. Giant Bull Kelp provides habitat and shelter for a variety of marine species, contributing to the rich coastal biodiversity.

Natural Features:

1. **Fiordland National Park:**

   Fiordland National Park, a UNESCO World Heritage site, is a captivating natural wonder that showcases breathtaking fjords, towering peaks, and cascading waterfalls. The history of Fiordland dates back thousands of years when glacial erosion sculpted its iconic landscapes. The park is home to Milford Sound, Doubtful Sound, and numerous other fiords that offer a surreal experience of sheer cliffs, lush rainforests, and pristine waters.

2. Aoraki/Mount Cook National Park:

Aoraki/Mount Cook National Park encompasses New Zealand's highest peak, Mount Cook, and its surrounding alpine beauty. The park holds great cultural significance for the indigenous Māori people and is steeped in legends and tales. The towering mountains, glaciers, and turquoise lakes paint a breathtaking canvas, attracting climbers, hikers, and nature enthusiasts from around the globe.

3. Franz Josef and Fox Glaciers:

The Franz Josef and Fox Glaciers are awe-inspiring natural wonders that have shaped the West Coast of South Island over centuries. These massive rivers of ice descend from the Southern Alps and wind their way through lush rainforests, creating a mesmerizing juxtaposition of icy blue and vibrant green. The history of these glaciers spans thousands of years, with their continuous movement carving out valleys and leaving behind remarkable geological formations.

4. Abel Tasman National Park:

Abel Tasman National Park is renowned for its pristine golden beaches, turquoise waters, and lush coastal forests. The park's history is intertwined with the Māori people, who have inhabited the region for centuries. The coastal cliffs, hidden coves, and offshore islands provide a picturesque setting for kayaking, hiking, and wildlife encounters. Abel Tasman National Park is a testament to the enduring beauty of New Zealand's coastal landscapes

Cultural Diversity and Heritage

This island is home to a multitude of ethnic communities, including Māori, European, Asian, and Pacific Islander cultures. The unique blend of these cultures has contributed to the formation of a vibrant tapestry of traditions, customs, and heritage that is deeply rooted in the history and identity of the South Island.

✦ Māori Culture:

Māori culture is an integral part of the South Island's identity, reflecting the deep connection of the Māori people to the land. Visitors to the South Island have the opportunity to immerse themselves in the richness of Māori traditions and customs. Exploring marae (traditional meeting grounds) allows one to experience the spiritual and communal heart of Māori culture. The powhiri (traditional welcome) offers insights into Māori protocols, including the hongi (pressing of noses) and speeches that acknowledge the importance of visitors. Cultural performances such as the haka (war dance) and waiata (songs) provide an engaging display of Māori identity and storytelling.

The South Island boasts significant Māori sites, such as Aoraki/Mount Cook, a sacred mountain in the Southern Alps, where ancestral connections and mythological narratives are deeply intertwined with the landscape. Another notable location is the Moeraki Boulders, large spherical rocks on Koekohe Beach, which hold both geological and cultural significance for the Māori people. These sites allow visitors to witness the spiritual connection Māori have with their environment and appreciate the rich oral traditions that have been passed down through generations.

2. **European Heritage**:

The European influence in the South Island dates back to the mid-19th century when European settlers arrived, bringing with them their traditions, languages, and customs. Their impact is evident in the architecture, historical landmarks, and the arts. Cities and towns throughout the South Island proudly showcase their European routes through the preservation of Victorian-era buildings, charming churches, and iconic structures like the Dunedin Railway Station, which is known for its stunning architectural design.

European settlers also brought their agricultural practices, which shaped the region's economy and contributed to its distinct character. Sheep farming, in particular, has become an integral part of the South Island's identity. Visitors can witness the beauty of vast pastoral landscapes dotted with grazing sheep, and they can even participate in farm tours to gain a deeper understanding of the farming heritage and the wool industry. Additionally, the South Island's viticulture industry, influenced by European winemaking traditions, has flourished, producing world-class wines that reflect the unique terroir of the region.

3. **Asian Communities:**

In recent decades, the South Island has experienced significant growth in its Asian population, contributing to the cultural diversity of the region. Asian communities have brought their own vibrant cultures, traditions, and culinary delights, enriching the South Island's cultural fabric. Cities like Christchurch and Queenstown offer a wide range of Asian dining experiences, from authentic Chinese, Japanese, and Korean cuisine to fusion options that showcase the blending of cultures. Asian supermarkets and specialty stores allow visitors and residents to explore and purchase a variety of ingredients and products that reflect the diverse Asian heritage.

Festivals also play a significant role in celebrating and promoting Asian cultures in the South Island. Events such as Chinese New Year and Diwali are celebrated with great enthusiasm, featuring vibrant parades, traditional performances, and cultural exhibitions. These festivals provide opportunities for cultural exchange, fostering a deeper appreciation and understanding of Asian traditions and customs among the wider community.

4. Pacific Island Influence:

The Pacific Islander communities have made a notable impact on the cultural diversity of the South Island, infusing it with their unique heritage and traditions. The Pacific Island influence can be observed in various aspects, including music, dance, cuisine, and art. Pacific Island communities often organize cultural events that showcase their vibrant dances, music, and traditional attire. These events offer visitors a chance to witness the joyous and energetic expressions of Pacific Island culture.

Food is another area where the Pacific Island influence is evident. Visitors can savour traditional Pacific Island cuisine, such as the mouth-watering flavours of Tongan, Samoan, and Fijian dishes. Festivals like Pasifika, which celebrates the diversity of Pacific Island cultures, are held in cities like Christchurch, attracting a wide audience and promoting cultural understanding and appreciation.

EUROPEAN HERITAGE

CHAPTER FOUR

Getting to and Around South Island

Transportation Options

New Zealand has an incredible landscape and choose from a variety of transportation options:

Air

The South Island is home to several major airports that serve as hubs for domestic and international flights. Christchurch International Airport, located in the largest city on the South Island, offers a wide range of domestic connections to destinations such as Auckland, Wellington, Queenstown, and Dunedin. It also serves as an international gateway, with flights to and from Australia and another country

Sea

The South Island of New Zealand offers a comprehensive sea transport service that allows travellers to navigate its stunning coastal waters, explore remote islands, and enjoy scenic cruises.

a. Ferry Services:

Ferry services are a popular mode of sea transport for both tourists and locals, providing convenient access to various destinations on the South Island. The Cook Strait, located between the North and South Islands, is traversed by several ferry operators, including Interislander and Bluebridge, offering reliable and frequent crossings between Wellington on the North Island and Picton on the South Island.

The ferry journey across the Cook Strait is renowned for its breath-taking scenery, as it winds through the picturesque Marlborough Sounds, with its lush forests, secluded bays, and dramatic coastline. Passengers can enjoy comfortable facilities onboard, including observation decks, cafes, and even premium lounges, making the journey an experience in itself.

b. Cruise and Charter Services:

The South Island is a prime destination for cruise enthusiasts, with various operators offering a range of cruise experiences. Milford Sound, located in Fiordland National Park, is one of the most popular cruise destinations, where visitors can immerse themselves in the grandeur of towering cliffs, cascading waterfalls, and serene waters. Operators like Real Journeys and Southern Discoveries provide unforgettable cruises through this iconic fjord.

Other scenic cruises can be enjoyed in the Marlborough Sounds, where visitors can explore the pristine waterways, encounter diverse marine life, and indulge in wine tasting at the region's renowned vineyards. Cruise options are available from Picton, including eco-cruises and wildlife tours, allowing travelers to experience the unique beauty of this coastal paradise.

In addition to scheduled cruises, charter services are available for private excursions and customized itineraries. These charters offer flexibility and personalized experiences, catering to individual preferences and group sizes. Whether it's exploring remote islands, fishing in abundant waters, or embarking on multi-day expeditions, charter services provide a unique way to discover the hidden gems of the South Island's coastline.

c. **Island Hopping and Water Taxis:**

The South Island boasts several picturesque islands that are accessible via sea transport. For instance, the

Marlborough Sounds are home to islands like Queen Charlotte, D'Urville, and Stewart Island/Rakiura, each offering its own charm and recreational opportunities. Water taxi services operate in these regions, providing convenient transfers between mainland ports and island destinations. These water taxis allow visitors to hop between islands, explore secluded beaches, and access hiking trails, making it easier to experience the diverse landscapes and wildlife of the South Island's coastal areas.

Furthermore, water taxis are also available in other coastal towns like Akaroa and Kaikoura, where they serve as a means of transportation for wildlife encounters, such as swimming with dolphins or whale watching tours. These services offer a unique and immersive experience, combining sea transport with unforgettable wildlife encounters.

The sea transport service in the South Island provides travellers with diverse options to explore its coastal wonders, from ferry services that connect the island to the North Island, to scenic cruises through majestic fjords, and island-hopping adventures. With a range of sea transport options available, visitors can tailor their journey to their interests and create unforgettable memories as they navigate the pristine waters surrounding the South Island.

Land

The South Island of New Zealand offers a comprehensive and efficient land transport service, providing travellers with various options to explore its stunning landscapes, charming towns, and iconic attractions.

a. **Road Network:** The South Island boasts a well-developed road network, making it ideal for road trips and self-guided exploration. State Highways connect major cities and towns, allowing visitors to easily navigate between destinations. The roads are well-maintained, offering smooth and comfortable journeys while showcasing the region's breath-taking scenery.

The South Island is renowned for its iconic driving routes, including the Southern Scenic Route, which encompasses the Catlins, Fiordland, and the Southern Lakes. The West Coast is traversed by the Great Coast Road, offering breath-taking views of rugged coastlines and rainforests. The Alpine

Pacific Triangle takes travellers through the alpine landscapes of Hanmer Springs, the vineyards of Waipara, and the coastal beauty of Kaikoura.

Rental car services are readily available at major airports and towns, allowing visitors to explore the South Island at their own pace. Additionally, numerous tour operators are offering guided road trips, providing informative commentary and ensuring a hassle-free experience for those who prefer not to drive.

b. **Bus and Coach Services:** The South Island has a reliable and extensive bus and coach network, catering to both domestic and international travelers. Companies like InterCity and Naked Bus operate frequent services between major cities and towns, offering a cost-effective and convenient mode of transportation.

These bus services connect popular tourist destinations, including Queenstown, Christchurch, Dunedin, Nelson, and more, making it easy for travelers to hop between regions. The buses are comfortable and equipped with amenities such as Wi-Fi, air conditioning, and panoramic windows, ensuring a pleasant journey while admiring the picturesque landscapes.

Guided coach tours are also available, providing visitors with the opportunity to sit back, relax, and enjoy the scenery while an experienced guide shares insights about the South Island's history, culture, and natural wonders. These tours often include popular attractions, such as Milford Sound, Mount Cook, and the Franz Josef Glacier, allowing travelers to make the most of their time in the region.

c. **Railway Services:** Rail travel in the South Island offers a unique and scenic way to experience stunning landscapes. The TranzAlpine, one of New Zealand's most famous train journeys, traverses the Southern Alps between Christchurch and Greymouth. Passengers are treated to panoramic views of snow-capped mountains, pristine rivers, and vast plains, providing a memorable and immersive experience.

Other notable rail journeys include the Coastal Pacific, which runs between Christchurch and Picton, offering breath-taking views of the rugged Kaikoura coastline and the Marlborough wine region. These rail services provide a comfortable and leisurely option for travellers who wish to enjoy the South Island's landscapes without the need for driving.

Public Transportation

Buses

+ **InterCity**:

InterCity is a leading bus company in New Zealand, offering extensive services throughout the South Island. Their modern fleet of buses provides comfortable seating, ample legroom, and large windows, ensuring passengers can enjoy the scenic beauty along the way. InterCity operates regular services between major cities and towns, including Christchurch, Queenstown, Dunedin, Nelson, and more.

With InterCity, travellers have the flexibility to hop on and off at different locations, allowing them to tailor their itinerary and explore various attractions. The company's reliable schedules and affordable fares make it an excellent choice for budget-conscious travellers who want to experience the South Island's beauty at their own pace.

✦ **Naked Bus:** Naked Bus is another popular bus service operating in the South Island, offering a budget-friendly option for travellers. Despite its affordable prices, Naked Bus maintains a high level of comfort and service. Their buses are equipped with comfortable seating, air conditioning, and Wi-Fi, ensuring a pleasant journey while staying connected.

Naked Bus operates routes that cover major cities and towns in the South Island, providing travellers with convenient access to popular destinations and attractions. Their flexible ticketing options allow passengers to book one-way or return tickets, making it easy to customize their travel plans. With its affordability and reliability, Naked Bus appeals to both backpackers and budget travellers seeking a convenient and cost-effective mode of transportation.

- **Guided Coach Tours:** For travellers who prefer a guided and hassle-free experience, several companies offer captivating guided coach tours on the South Island. These tours provide the perfect opportunity to sit back, relax, and soak in the beauty of the region while an experienced guide shares insights and stories about the South Island's history, culture, and natural wonders.

Companies like GreatSights, New Zealand Coach Tours, and Kiwi Experience offer a range of guided coach tours, catering to different interests and durations. These tours often include popular attractions, such as Milford Sound, Mount Cook, the Franz Josef Glacier, and the stunning Queenstown region. Travelers can choose from day trips to multi-day adventures, allowing them to explore the South Island's highlights without the need for planning and navigating.

Guided coach tours provide a comfortable and social environment for travellers, allowing them to connect with like-minded individuals and forge new friendships along the way. With knowledgeable guides and well-planned itineraries, these tours offer a compelling and stress-free way to discover the South Island's diverse landscapes and hidden gems.

Trains

The South Island of New Zealand offers captivating train journeys that allow travellers to experience the region's stunning landscapes and scenic beauty

+ **TranzAlpine**: The TranzAlpine is one of the most renowned train journeys in New Zealand and is a must-do for any visitor to the South Island. This scenic train ride takes passengers on a breath-taking journey across the Southern Alps, showcasing the diverse landscapes of the South Island.

Starting from Christchurch, the Tranz Alpine crosses vast plains, meanders through river gorges, and ascends into the majestic Southern Alps. Passengers are treated to panoramic views of snow-capped mountains, alpine meadows, and turquoise rivers as they traverse the Arthur's Pass National Park. The train then descends through the rainforests of the West Coast, offering glimpses of cascading waterfalls and lush valleys before reaching its final destination in Greymouth.

The TranzAlpine features comfortable seating, large panoramic windows, and open-air viewing carriages, allowing passengers to fully immerse themselves in the awe-inspiring landscapes. With informative commentary, onboard amenities, and the option to purchase food and beverages, the TranzAlpine provides a captivating and luxurious way to experience the South Island's natural wonders.

✦ **Coastal Pacific:** The Coastal Pacific is another remarkable train journey that showcases the beauty of the South Island's eastern coastline. This scenic rail route travels from Christchurch to Picton, passing through stunning coastal landscapes, rolling vineyards, and charming seaside towns.

The Coastal Pacific offers passengers panoramic views of the Pacific Ocean as the train hugs the coastline. Travelers can admire the rugged Kaikoura coastline, known for its marine wildlife, including whales and dolphins. The journey continues through the picturesque Marlborough wine region, famous for its vineyards and cellar doors. Finally, the train reaches Picton, a gateway to the beautiful Marlborough Sounds.

The Coastal Pacific features comfortable seating, large windows, and open-air viewing carriages, allowing passengers to take in the coastal vistas and capture memorable photographs. Onboard services include informative commentary, a café serving local cuisine, and Wi-Fi connectivity, ensuring a pleasant and enriching journey.

Taxis

The South Island of New Zealand offers a variety of taxi services that provide convenient and reliable transportation options for travellers

+ **Conventional Taxis:** Conventional taxis are readily available in major cities and towns throughout the South Island. These taxis can be hailed on the street or found at designated taxi stands. They provide a convenient and efficient mode of transportation, offering door-to-door service for individuals or small groups.

Conventional taxis in the South Island are usually metered, ensuring transparent pricing based on distance travelled and waiting time. Taxi drivers are professional and knowledgeable about the local area, making them a valuable resource for travellers seeking recommendations or information about the region.

+ **Ride-Hailing Services:** Ride-hailing services, such as Uber and Ola, have gained popularity in the South Island, offering an alternative to traditional taxis. These services can be accessed through smartphone applications, allowing travellers to request a ride and track their driver's arrival in real time.

Ride-hailing services in the South Island provide convenience, competitive pricing, and a seamless booking experience. They often offer a range of vehicle options, including standard sedans, larger vehicles for groups, and even luxury cars for special occasions. These services are particularly convenient for travellers who prefer cashless payments and the convenience of booking a ride from anywhere at any time.

- **Shuttle Services**: Shuttle services are another popular transportation option in the South Island, especially for airport transfers or group travel. Shuttle companies operate scheduled services between airports and major towns, providing shared transportation at fixed rates. These services are cost-effective, as the fare is divided among passengers sharing the same route.

Shuttle services offer convenience, reliability, and the opportunity to meet fellow travellers. They typically operate on a pre-booked basis, allowing passengers to secure their seats in advance and avoid any waiting time. Shuttle drivers are knowledgeable about the local area, often providing informative commentary along the way.

+ **Water Taxis:** In coastal regions, such as the Marlborough Sounds, water taxis are a unique form of transportation. These taxis transport passengers across the stunning waterways, connecting remote areas and providing access to hiking trails, beaches, and secluded bays.

Water taxis in the South Island offer an exciting and scenic way to travel, combining transportation with the opportunity to appreciate the region's coastal beauty. They are particularly popular in areas like Picton and Nelson, where they provide transfers to remote islands, wildlife encounters, and access to the Marlborough Sounds' stunning landscapes.

Car Rentals and Driving Tips

Renting a car is a popular and convenient option for exploring the stunning landscapes and charming towns of the South Island in New Zealand.

+ **Car Rental Services:** Major car rental companies, such as Hertz, Avis, Budget, and Thrifty, operate in the South Island, offering a wide range of vehicles to suit various needs and budgets. These rental services are available at major airports, including Christchurch, Queenstown, and Dunedin, as well as in city centres and other popular tourist destinations.

When renting a car, it is advisable to book in advance, especially during peak travel seasons, to secure the vehicle of your choice. Most rental companies provide online booking options, allowing you to compare prices and select the most suitable vehicle for your trip.

- **Driving License and Requirements:** To rent and drive a car in New Zealand, visitors must have a valid driving license written in English. If your license is not in English, you will need to carry an international driving permit (IDP) alongside your original license.

It is important to note that in New Zealand, vehicles drive on the left side of the road. If you are unfamiliar with driving on the left, take some time to get acclimated before embarking on longer journeys. Additionally, the legal driving age in New Zealand is 16 years for a learner's license and 18 years for a full driver's license.

- **Road Rules and Safety**: Familiarize yourself with New Zealand's Road rules and regulations to ensure a safe and enjoyable driving experience. Here are some key points to keep in mind:

  - **Speed Limits:** Speed limits are clearly signposted and generally range from 50 km/h (31 mph) in urban areas to 100 km/h (62 mph) on open roads unless otherwise specified. Always adhere to the posted speed limits and adjust your speed according to road and weather conditions.

  - **Seat Belts**: Seat belts must be worn by all passengers, including those seated in the back of the vehicle. Children under seven years of age must be securely restrained in an approved child restraint appropriate for their age and size.

  - **Alcohol and Drug Limits:** It is illegal to drive under the influence of alcohol or drugs in New Zealand. The legal blood alcohol concentration (BAC) limit is 0.05%, and random breath tests are conducted by the police to ensure compliance.

- **Mobile Phone Usage:** It is prohibited to use a handheld mobile phone while driving. If you need to use your phone, pull over in a safe and designated area.

- **Road Conditions:** The South Island's roads vary from highways to narrow and winding mountain roads. Take extra caution when driving on rural roads, especially in remote areas, and be aware of changing weather conditions.

4. **Plan Your Itinerary:** Before setting off on your journey, plan your itinerary and consider the distances and travel times between destinations. The South Island offers stunning landscapes, and you'll want to allocate enough time to fully enjoy each place you visit. Take into account any stops or attractions along the way to make the most of your trip.

5. **Fuel and Service Stations:** Ensure your rental car has a full tank of fuel before embarking on your journey, as service stations can be limited in remote areas. Plan your refueling stops accordingly, especially when traveling long distances or exploring more rural regions.

6. **Travel Insurance:** Consider obtaining travel insurance that includes coverage for rental car excess, in case of any unforeseen circumstances or accidents during your trip.

Cycling and Hiking Routes

South Island, New Zealand, is a paradise for outdoor enthusiasts, offering an array of awe-inspiring landscapes and thrilling adventures. From majestic mountains to crystal-clear lakes, dense forests to rugged coastlines, the South Island is a haven for cyclists and hikers alike. In this article, we will delve into some of the most compelling cycling and hiking routes that showcase the natural beauty and diversity of this remarkable region.

a. **The Queen Charlotte Track:** Nestled in the Marlborough Sounds, the Queen Charlotte Track is a renowned hiking and biking trail. This 70-kilometer journey meanders along the ridgeline, offering breath-taking vistas of the sounds, native bush, and secluded bays. With a well-maintained track and convenient accommodation options, adventurers can immerse themselves in this captivating coastal experience.

b. **The Otago Central Rail Trail:** For history enthusiasts and cycling aficionados, the Otago Central Rail Trail is a must-visit. Following the path of a former railway line, this 150-kilometer trail winds through the heart of Central Otago's picturesque landscapes. Traverse charming historic towns, viaducts, tunnels, and viaducts while relishing the region's unique gold mining heritage and stunning alpine scenery.

c. **Abel Tasman Coast Track:** Situated in Abel Tasman National Park, the Abel Tasman Coast Track is a coastal paradise for hikers and bikers. This 60-kilometer track boasts golden beaches, turquoise waters, and lush native forests. Traversing estuaries, rocky headlands, and peaceful bays, visitors can explore the park's hidden gems and encounter diverse wildlife, including fur seals and dolphins.

d. **The Route burn Track**: The Route Burn Track is a world-renowned hiking trail that spans the Southern Alps, connecting Fiordland and Mount Aspiring National Parks. Covering approximately 32 kilometers, this route offers awe-inspiring mountain vistas, dramatic alpine scenery, and pristine lakes. Adventurers can immerse themselves in the grandeur of nature while encountering waterfalls, snow-capped peaks, and diverse flora and fauna.

e. **The West Coast Wilderness Trail:** The West Coast Wilderness Trail provides an exceptional cycling experience through the untamed beauty of the South Island's West Coast. Stretching for 139 kilometres, this trail takes riders on a captivating journey through ancient rainforests, river valleys, and rugged coastlines. Experience the region's rich history, including remnants of gold mining and logging, while revelling in the solitude and serenity of the wild landscapes.

CHAPTER FIVE

Accommodation and Dining

Accommodation Options

There are various Accommodation options in South Island and are categorized as thus:

Hotels

As you embark on your journey through this enchanting region, let us guide you through some of the best hotel accommodations that will make your stay truly unforgettable.

1. **The Remarkable Lodge**: Nestled amidst the majestic Southern Alps, The Remarkable Lodge offers a luxurious escape surrounded by unparalleled natural beauty. This exclusive lodge combines rustic charm with modern amenities, providing a haven for relaxation and adventure. Indulge in gourmet cuisine, unwind in the spa, and soak in panoramic views of snow-capped mountains from your private balcony.

2. **Fiordland Wilderness Resort:** Located on the edge of the stunning Fiordland National Park, this resort immerses you in the wild beauty of South Island. Experience true tranquillity in their well-appointed cabins, blending seamlessly with the surrounding forest. From here, embark on awe-inspiring hikes, boat tours through Milford Sound, or simply revel in the serenity of nature.

3. **Blanket Bay:** Situated on the shores of Lake Wakatipu, Blanket Bay offers a secluded retreat where luxury meets wilderness. With its elegant rooms, gourmet dining, and world-class spa, this lodge provides an idyllic sanctuary for discerning travellers. Engage in thrilling activities like heli-skiing, jet boating, or simply unwind with a glass of local wine while admiring the breath taking alpine vistas.

4. **Hapuku Lodge & Tree Houses:** For a unique and unforgettable experience, Hapuku Lodge & Tree Houses will capture your imagination. Nestled amidst a working deer farm, this eco-friendly retreat features luxurious treehouses perched high among the treetops. Immerse yourself in the sounds and scents of the forest, savour gourmet farm-to-table cuisine, and enjoy activities such as whale watching or exploring the nearby Kaikoura Peninsula.

5. **Otahuna Lodge:** Set within an 1895 Victorian mansion, Otahuna Lodge offers a luxurious escape in the heart of the Canterbury countryside. Surrounded by beautiful gardens and rolling hills, this lodge combines historic elegance with contemporary comforts. Indulge in exquisite cuisine crafted from local produce, relax in the heated pool, or explore the nearby vineyards and art galleries.

6. **The Rees Hotel:** Overlooking the tranquil waters of Lake Wakatipu, The Rees Hotel is a modern and sophisticated retreat in Queenstown. Its spacious and stylish suites boast breath taking lake and mountain views, while the attentive service ensures a truly personalized experience. Take advantage of the hotel's private beach, award-winning restaurant, and convenient access to the town's vibrant attractions.

7. **Marlborough Vintners Hotel**: If you're a wine enthusiast, the Marlborough Vintners Hotel is the perfect base for exploring New Zealand's renowned wine region. Surrounded by vineyards and lush gardens, this boutique hotel offers elegant suites with private balconies, allowing you to savour the breath-taking scenery. Discover the region's world-class wineries, indulge in gourmet cuisine, and relax in the hotel's outdoor pool and spa.

8. **The Hermitage Hotel:** Situated in the heart of Aoraki/Mount Cook National Park, The Hermitage Hotel is an iconic landmark offering awe-inspiring views of New Zealand's highest peak, Mount Cook. This historic hotel combines old-world charm with modern amenities, featuring comfortable rooms and suites designed to make your stay unforgettable. Enjoy fine dining at the on-site restaurant, embark on scenic hikes, or stargaze under the incredibly clear night sky.

9. **Azur Lodge:** Perched high on a hillside in Queenstown, Azur Lodge offers a luxurious retreat with breath-taking panoramic views of Lake Wakatipu and the surrounding mountains. Each private villa features floor-to-ceiling windows, allowing you to immerse yourself in the natural beauty of the region. Indulge in personalized service, unwind in your private spa, and enjoy the serenity of this intimate and exclusive escape.

10. **Millbrook Resort:** Located in Arrowtown, just a short drive from Queenstown, Millbrook Resort is a world-class destination offering a wide range of accommodation options to suit every traveler. From spacious villas to elegant hotel rooms, this resort provides a peaceful and picturesque setting surrounded by rolling hills and championship golf courses. Pamper yourself at the spa, dine at award-winning restaurants, and explore the nearby historic town of Arrowtown.

11. **Te Waonui Forest Retreat:** Tucked away in the lush rainforest of Franz Josef, Te Waonui Forest Retreat immerses you in the natural beauty of the West Coast. The eco-friendly retreat offers spacious and modern rooms with private balconies, allowing you to connect with nature from the comfort of your own sanctuary. Unwind at the on-site spa, discover the nearby Franz Josef Glacier, or take a stroll through the enchanting forest.

12. **Eichardt's Private Hotel:** Situated on the shores of Lake Wakatipu in Queenstown, Eichardt's Private Hotel is a luxurious boutique accommodation renowned for its elegance and sophistication. Choose from beautifully appointed suites or the exclusive Eichardt's Residence, all exuding timeless charm and offering stunning lake and mountain views. Delight in gourmet dining, sip on handcrafted cocktails at the bar, and experience the vibrant atmosphere of Queenstown right at your doorstep.

13. **The George:** Located in the heart of Christchurch, The George is an exquisite boutique hotel renowned for its impeccable service and attention to detail. Offering a combination of timeless elegance and contemporary style, this hotel boasts luxurious rooms and suites, many of which overlook the tranquil Hagley Park. Indulge in culinary delights at the on-site restaurant, relax in the elegant lounge, or explore the vibrant city center just moments away.

14. **Peppers Bluewater Resort:** Set against the stunning backdrop of Lake Tekapo, Peppers Bluewater Resort offers a serene retreat in the Mackenzie Basin. Choose from well-appointed rooms or spacious self-contained apartments, each designed to provide the utmost comfort and relaxation. Immerse yourself in the soothing waters of the on-site hot

pools, stargaze at the nearby Mount John Observatory, or simply unwind and take in the beauty of the turquoise lake.

15. **The Marlborough Lodge**: Surrounded by vineyards and gardens in the heart of the Marlborough wine region, The Marlborough Lodge is a boutique retreat that exudes elegance and charm. Set within a historic Victorian convent, this lodge offers luxurious suites, gourmet cuisine, and warm hospitality. Explore the renowned wineries of Marlborough,

unwind in the tranquil gardens, or partake in outdoor activities such as biking or kayaking.

B&Bs

As you embark on your journey through this captivating region, let us guide you through some of the best B&Bs that will make your stay truly unforgettable.

1. **Fyffe Country Lodge:** Nestled in the picturesque Kaikoura region, Fyffe Country Lodge offers a tranquil retreat surrounded by stunning mountain vistas and sweeping coastal views. This elegant B&B features spacious and beautifully appointed rooms, each with its private balcony or patio. Indulge in a delicious homemade breakfast, relax in the garden, and enjoy the warm

hospitality of the hosts who will ensure your stay is memorable.

2. **Olivers Central Otago**: Located in the heart of historic Clyde, Olivers Central Otago is a charming B&B that seamlessly blends heritage charm with modern comfort. Housed in a beautifully restored historic building, this boutique accommodation offers tastefully decorated rooms, a cozy lounge with a fireplace, and a delightful on-site restaurant serving locally sourced cuisine. Immerse yourself in the rich history of the area and explore the stunning Central Otago wine region.

3. **The Mudcastle:** Set amidst the rolling hills of Tasman, The Mudcastle is a unique and enchanting B&B that provides a truly memorable experience. This fairytale-like castle offers luxurious suites adorned with handcrafted mud bricks, elegant furnishings, and private balconies overlooking the surrounding vineyards and mountains. Enjoy a sumptuous breakfast, stroll through the beautiful gardens, or simply unwind in the opulent surroundings.

4. **Huntley House:** Situated in the vibrant city of Christchurch, Huntley House is a charming B&B that combines comfort and convenience. This beautifully restored Victorian villa offers well-appointed rooms with elegant decor and modern amenities. Start your day with a delicious homemade breakfast before exploring the city's attractions, such as the Botanic Gardens or the bustling Christchurch Art Gallery.

5. **The Old Manse:** Located in the charming town of Clyde, The Old Manse is a delightful B&B housed in a historic Victorian villa. The beautifully furnished rooms exude old-world charm, while the tranquil gardens provide a serene setting for relaxation. Enjoy a hearty breakfast made with locally sourced ingredients and take advantage of the proximity to Central Otago's renowned cycling trails and vineyards.

6. **The Barn Bed & Breakfast:** Tucked away in the idyllic countryside near Akaroa, The Barn Bed & Breakfast offers a peaceful escape surrounded by natural beauty. This rustic yet elegant B&B features cozy rooms with wood-beamed ceilings and stunning views of the surrounding farmland. Wake up to a delicious breakfast

made with fresh local produce and spend your days exploring the charming town of Akaroa or relaxing on the nearby beaches.

7. **Ferryman's Cottage:** Set in the picturesque town of Arrowtown, Ferryman's Cottage is a charming B&B that captures the essence of the region's gold rush history. This quaint cottage offers comfortable rooms with antique furnishings, a lovely garden for relaxation, and a delicious homemade breakfast to start your day. Explore the town's heritage sites, go for a hike in the nearby mountains, or simply enjoy the peaceful ambiance of this historic retreat.

8. **Pen-y-Bryn Lodge:** Located in the charming town of Oamaru, Pen-y-bryn Lodge is a grand Victorian mansion that offers a luxurious and intimate B&B experience. This heritage-listed property features beautifully appointed rooms with elegant decor, antique furnishings, and modern amenities. Enjoy a gourmet breakfast served in the elegant dining room, relax in the cozy library, or take a stroll through the enchanting gardens.

9. **Awatea Tasman Bay**: Situated in the sunny Nelson region, Awatea Tasman Bay is a boutique B&B that provides a peaceful and idyllic retreat. Nestled amongst olive groves and vineyards, this elegant accommodation offers spacious rooms with private balconies or patios offering panoramic views of the Tasman Bay. Start your day with a delicious breakfast featuring locally sourced ingredients and explore the nearby wineries, golden beaches, and stunning national parks.

10. **The Turret B&B:** Located in the heart of Queenstown, The Turret B&B is a charming and historic property that offers a cozy and welcoming atmosphere. The beautifully restored villa features comfortable rooms with unique characters, and the friendly hosts ensure a personalized and memorable stay. Enjoy a hearty homemade breakfast, take in the breathtaking views of Lake Wakatipu, and explore the vibrant town center just a short walk away.

11. **Braemar on Parliament Street**: Situated in the vibrant city of Dunedin, Braemar on Parliament Street is a boutique B&B that combines elegance with modern comforts. Set in a beautifully restored Victorian mansion, this luxurious accommodation offers individually styled

rooms, sumptuous breakfasts, and warm hospitality. Explore the city's rich heritage, visit the stunning Otago Peninsula, or simply relax in the charming surroundings of this exquisite B&B.

12. **Rosneath Bed and Breakfast:** Set in the heart of historic Akaroa, Rosneath Bed and Breakfast is a delightful colonial-style property that exudes charm and tranquility. The cozy rooms feature antique furnishings and offer views of the garden or the harbor. Wake up to a delicious homemade breakfast and spend your days exploring the French-inspired village, taking a cruise on the harbor, or indulging in the local cuisine.

13. **The Mussel Bed Boutique B&B**: Located in Havelock, the gateway to the beautiful Marlborough Sounds, The Mussel Bed Boutique B&B offers a peaceful and scenic retreat. This cozy accommodation features comfortable rooms, a lovely garden, and warm hospitality. Start your day with a delicious breakfast showcasing local produce, embark on a scenic boat trip to explore the sounds, or simply relax and soak in the serene atmosphere.

14. **Punga Cove Resort:** Nestled in the stunning Marlborough Sounds, Punga Cove Resort offers a unique B&B experience amidst pristine natural surroundings. This eco-friendly resort features charming guestrooms and self-contained units, all with breathtaking views of the bay. Enjoy a delicious breakfast at the on-site restaurant, go kayaking or hiking in the surrounding wilderness, or simply unwind on the secluded beach.

15. **Marlborough Bed and Breakfast:** Set in the heart of the Marlborough wine region, Marlborough Bed and Breakfast provides a comfortable and welcoming base for exploring the area's renowned vineyards. This family-run B&B offers tastefully decorated rooms, a delicious homemade breakfast, and personalized service. Take a leisurely bike ride through the vineyards, indulge in wine tastings, or simply relax in the peaceful garden.

Campgrounds

let us introduce you to some of the best campgrounds that will allow you to fully embrace the region's natural wonders.

1. **Lake Wanaka DOC Campsite:** Located on the shores of stunning Lake Wanaka, this Department of

Conservation (DOC) campsite offers breathtaking views and a tranquil setting. Set up your tent or park your camper van and wake up to the serene beauty of the lake surrounded by majestic mountains. Enjoy swimming, fishing, or simply relaxing by the campfire as you take in the incredible scenery.

2. **Abel Tasman National Park Campgrounds:** As one of New Zealand's most beloved national parks, Abel Tasman is a coastal paradise offering several campgrounds nestled along its beautiful coastline. With options ranging from basic campsites to more equipped facilities, you can choose your preferred level of comfort. Spend your days hiking through lush forests, exploring golden sandy beaches, and kayaking along crystal-clear waters.

3. **Aoraki/Mount Cook National Park Campgrounds:** Immerse yourself in the awe-inspiring beauty of Aoraki/Mount Cook National Park by camping in one of the campgrounds within the park. Marvel at the majestic peaks and glaciers surrounding you as you pitch your tent or park your campervan. Take advantage of the numerous

hiking trails, guided tours, and stargazing opportunities for an unforgettable camping adventure.

4. **Queenstown Lakeview Holiday Park**: Situated just a short distance from Queenstown, this holiday park offers stunning views of Lake Wakatipu and the surrounding mountains. Choose from powered or non-powered sites and enjoy the range of amenities including kitchen facilities, BBQ areas, and communal spaces. Experience the thrill of adventure activities in Queenstown, or simply unwind in the beautiful natural surroundings.

5. **Mount Aspiring National Park Campgrounds:** Located near Wanaka, Mount Aspiring National Park is a pristine wilderness known for its rugged beauty and diverse landscapes. The park offers several campgrounds, providing a chance to immerse yourself in the tranquility of the alpine environment. Engage in hiking, fishing, or wildlife spotting as you discover the untouched beauty of this remarkable national park.

6. **Catlins Forest Park Campgrounds**: If you're seeking a camping experience amidst lush forests, rugged coastlines, and cascading waterfalls, Catlins Forest Park

is the perfect destination. Choose from various campgrounds throughout the park, each offering a unique natural setting. Explore the stunning coastline, encounter wildlife such as seals and penguins, and be captivated by the region's untamed beauty.

7. **Fiordland National Park Campgrounds:** As one of New Zealand's largest national parks, Fiordland offers a range of campgrounds amidst its dramatic landscapes. From Milford Sound to Doubtful Sound, you can find campsites that provide a front-row seat to the park's stunning fjords, mountains, and pristine wilderness. Immerse yourself in the serenity of the surroundings, embark on unforgettable hikes, and experience the magic of Fiordland.

8. **Golden Bay Campgrounds:** Located in the scenic Golden Bay area, you'll find a variety of campgrounds offering a chance to experience the beauty of this coastal paradise. From remote beachfront campsites to family-friendly holiday parks, you can choose the perfect spot to enjoy the golden sandy beaches, clear turquoise waters, and the relaxed atmosphere of this idyllic region.

9. **West Coast Wilderness Campgrounds:** The West Coast of the South Island is renowned for its untamed beauty and rugged landscapes. Experience the raw wilderness by camping in one of the campgrounds scattered along the coast. Wake up to the sound of crashing waves, explore ancient rainforests, and witness stunning sunsets over the Tasman Sea as you immerse yourself in the wild allure of the West Coast.

10. **Nelson Lakes National Park Campgrounds:** Nestled within the Southern Alps, Nelson Lakes National Park offers a tranquil camping experience surrounded by pristine lakes and majestic mountains. Choose from a variety of campgrounds and enjoy activities such as hiking, fishing, and boating. Marvel at the mirror-like reflections of the mountains on the lakes, breathe in the fresh alpine air, and immerse yourself in the beauty of this alpine wonderland.

Dining Experiences

Local Cuisine and Restaurant Recommendations

Join us as we explore some of the best local cuisine and restaurant recommendations in South Island.

1. **Fleur's Place (Moeraki):** Located in the picturesque fishing village of Moeraki, Fleur's Place is a renowned seafood restaurant that showcases the freshest local catch. Enjoy their signature dishes such as blue cod, crayfish, and oysters sourced directly from the nearby waters. With a rustic and charming atmosphere, Fleur's Place offers a truly authentic and unforgettable dining experience.

2. **Pegasus Bay Winery and Restaurant (Waipara):** Situated in the heart of the Waipara wine region, Pegasus Bay Winery and Restaurant is a culinary gem known for its elegant cuisine and award-winning wines. The restaurant showcases local and seasonal produce, with dishes that beautifully complement their exceptional wines. Indulge in a degustation menu paired with their renowned Pinot Noir or Riesling for a truly memorable experience.

3. **Roots Restaurant (Lyttelton):** Housed in a restored 1930s villa in the charming port town of Lyttelton, Roots Restaurant offers an innovative and seasonally driven dining experience. The talented chefs create a constantly evolving menu that highlights the region's finest ingredients, often foraged or sourced from local farmers. Immerse yourself in their unique culinary journey that celebrates the flavors of South Island.

4. **Botswana Butchery (Queenstown):** Located on the picturesque waterfront of Queenstown, Botswana Butchery is a premier steak and seafood restaurant that showcases the best of local and international cuisine. From succulent New Zealand lamb to fresh seafood delights, their menu offers a range of tantalizing options. The elegant atmosphere, attentive service, and stunning lake views make for an exceptional dining experience.

5. **Pātaka Kai (Kaikoura):** Set in the charming coastal town of Kaikoura, Pātaka Kai is a unique food truck experience that celebrates the local Maori culture and culinary traditions. The menu features a fusion of indigenous flavors and modern techniques, offering dishes such as kaimoana (seafood), wild game, and

traditional hangi (earth oven) preparations. Immerse yourself in the rich cultural heritage and culinary delights of New Zealand's indigenous people.

6. **The Herb Farm (Ashhurst):** Situated in the beautiful Manawatu region, The Herb Farm is a culinary destination that embraces the concept of farm-to-table dining. Set in an idyllic garden setting, the restaurant offers a menu crafted with fresh herbs and seasonal produce grown on-site. Experience the flavors of their herb-infused dishes, relax in the tranquil surroundings, and explore the adjacent gardens and gift shops.

7. **Fiddlesticks Restaurant and Bar (Christchurch):** Located in the heart of Christchurch, Fiddlesticks is a popular dining spot that showcases the best of local and international cuisine. With a focus on fresh and seasonal ingredients, their menu offers a wide range of dishes, from seafood and steaks to vegetarian options. The warm and inviting atmosphere, coupled with attentive service, makes for a delightful dining experience.

8. **The Jolly Potter (Hanmer Springs):** Situated in the picturesque alpine village of Hanmer Springs, The Jolly

Potter is a beloved local institution known for its hearty pub-style fare. Feast on classic New Zealand dishes such as lamb shanks, fish and chips, or a delicious gourmet burger. Enjoy the cozy atmosphere, friendly hospitality, and perhaps indulge in a pint of locally brewed craft beer.

9. **Fyffe and Barrel (Kaikoura):** Combining the flavors of South Island with a touch of international inspiration, Fyffe and Barrel in Kaikoura offers a delightful fusion of cuisine. From locally sourced seafood to globally influenced dishes, their menu offers something for every palate. With a relaxed and welcoming ambiance, this restaurant is a perfect stop for a satisfying meal after exploring the beauty of Kaikoura.

10. **Jervois Steak House (Queenstown):** For the discerning carnivore, Jervois Steak House in Queenstown is a must-visit. This premier steakhouse sources the finest New Zealand beef, dry-aging it in-house to achieve exceptional flavor and tenderness. Indulge in a perfectly cooked steak accompanied by classic sides and a carefully curated wine list.

CHAPTER SIX

Exploring South Island's Cities

New Zealand's South Island is an idyllic sanctuary for those captivated by nature's wonders and thrill-seekers alike. Its awe-inspiring landscapes encompass majestic peaks and glistening shorelines, forming a picturesque setting to delve into the vibrant metropolises dotting the region. Whether you revel in outdoor pursuits, embark on a cultural odyssey, or simply yearn for serenity amidst breath-taking environs, the South Island presents an array of enticing possibilities to cater to all.

Christchurch

Christchurch, situated on the picturesque east coast of New Zealand's South Island, is a city that unveils a captivating history, a myriad of attractions, and a vibrant culinary scene. From its Maori heritage to the transformative events that have shaped its identity, Christchurch offers an educational and enriching experience for visitors. In this article, we delve into the unique history of Christchurch, explore its top attractions, and indulge in the diverse dining options that make it a culinary haven.

History

✦ Maori Origins

Before European settlement, the area now known as Christchurch was inhabited by the Ngāi Tahu, a prominent Maori tribe. Their deep connection to the land is evident in the names of local landmarks and the rich cultural heritage that still resonates in the city today. To explore the Maori history, a visit to the Ngā Puna Wai Sports Hub is recommended, where you can learn about ancestral connections and engage in cultural activities.

✦ European Settlement

The story of Christchurch as a European settlement began in 1848 when the Canterbury Association, led by John Robert Godley, arrived with the vision of establishing an Anglican colony. The city was named Christchurch in honor of Christ Church, one of the Association's influential members. Discover the city's colonial past by visiting the Canterbury Museum, which showcases artifacts and exhibits that chronicle the early days of European settlement.

- **Earthquakes and Resilience:**

  Christchurch has faced significant challenges, most notably the devastating earthquakes of 2010 and 2011 that caused widespread destruction. Despite the tragedy, the city has showcased remarkable resilience in its rebuilding efforts. The Quake City exhibition offers a poignant insight into the earthquakes and their impact, highlighting the strength and determination of the people of Christchurch.

Attractions

- **Christchurch Botanic Gardens**

  The Christchurch Botanic Gardens offer a serene escape into nature. Explore the diverse range of plants, stroll along the winding paths, and relax amidst the beauty of the conservatories. The Gardens also feature the charming Antigua Boat Sheds, where you can rent a paddleboat and leisurely explore the Avon River.

- **Canterbury Museum**

  Immerse yourself in the city's history and cultural heritage at the Canterbury Museum. Discover captivating exhibitions, including the Maori Galleries, Antarctic displays, and the natural history collection. From ancient artifacts to contemporary artworks, the museum offers a comprehensive exploration of the region's past and present.

- **International Antarctic Centre:**
  For an unforgettable adventure, visit the International Antarctic Centre, a world-renowned facility dedicated to showcasing the wonders of the Antarctic. Experience a simulated Antarctic storm, meet adorable penguins, and learn about the intrepid explorers who braved the icy continent. The centre also offers informative exhibits on climate change and conservation.

Dining

- **The Arts Centre Market**

Immerse yourself in the bustling atmosphere of the Arts Centre Market, where local artisans, farmers, and food vendors come together to create a vibrant tapestry of flavor. Sample fresh produce, artisanal cheeses, and delectable street food while exploring the beautifully restored heritage buildings.

New Regent Street

Step back in time and indulge in the charm of New Regent Street, a pedestrian-only precinct lined with pastel-colored heritage buildings. This iconic street is home to an array of cafes, restaurants, and bars offering an eclectic mix of cuisines, from contemporary New Zealand dishes to international delights.

Little High Eatery

For a culinary adventure, visit the Little High Eatery, a lively dining destination that brings together a collection of diverse and innovative eateries under one roof. From Asian street food to gourmet burgers, there is something to satisfy every palate. Grab a seat, sample a variety of dishes, and savour the vibrant atmosphere.

Queenstown

Queenstown, situated amidst the awe-inspiring landscapes of New Zealand's South Island, is a destination that truly embodies the spirit of adventure. With its adrenaline-pumping adventure sports, breathtaking scenic beauty, and vibrant entertainment scene, Queenstown offers a truly immersive and captivating experience. In this article, we embark on a journey through the unique offerings of Queenstown, exploring its thrilling adventure sports, mesmerizing natural beauty, and exciting entertainment options.

Adventure Sports

✦ Bungee Jumping

Experience the ultimate adrenaline rush with a bungee jump in Queenstown, the birthplace of this extreme sport. Take the leap from the iconic Kawarau Bridge, suspended above the crystal-clear waters of the Kawarau River. For the more adventurous, the Nevis Bungy offers a heart-stopping plunge from a staggering 134 meters, surrounded by awe-inspiring mountain scenery. Whether you're a daredevil seeking an unforgettable thrill or a first-timer looking to conquer your fears, bungee jumping in Queenstown is an experience like no other.

Skydiving:

Take to the skies and embark on a tandem skydiving adventure that will leave you breathless. Feel the rush of adrenaline as you soar above the majestic Southern Alps, with panoramic views of Lake Wakatipu below. Plunge into freefall from staggering heights and experience the exhilaration of a lifetime. Queenstown's unique combination of stunning landscapes and professional skydiving operators make it an ideal destination for adrenaline junkies seeking the ultimate skydiving experience.

Jet Boating:

Zoom across the pristine waters of the Shotover or Kawarau rivers on a thrilling jet boat ride. Hold on tight as you navigate through narrow canyons, perform exhilarating spins, and feel the refreshing spray of water on your face. Queenstown's jet boating experiences offer a unique blend of adventure, natural beauty, and adrenaline-pumping excitement, making it a must-do activity for visitors seeking an unforgettable aquatic adventure.

Scenic Beauty

+ **Remarkable Mountains:**

Prepare to be mesmerized by the Remarkable Mountain Range, an iconic backdrop that defines the beauty of Queenstown. These majestic peaks, often snow-capped, provide a breath-taking panorama that will leave you in awe. Take a scenic drive to the Remarkable Lookout or hike one of the many trails in the area to immerse yourself in the grandeur of these towering mountains.

+ **Milford Sound**

Embark on a mesmerizing journey to Milford Sound, one of New Zealand's most spectacular natural wonders. Cruise through the fjord, surrounded by towering cliffs, cascading waterfalls, and lush rainforests. Witness the dramatic landscapes that have earned Milford Sound its reputation as the "Eighth Wonder of the World." Be sure to keep an eye out for playful dolphins, seals, and penguins that call this pristine environment home.

+ **Lake Wakatipu**

Serenely nestled amidst the mountains, Lake Wakatipu showcases the mesmerizing beauty of Queenstown. Take a stroll along the lake's shores, rent a paddleboard or kayak, or embark on a scenic boat cruise. The ever-changing hues of the lake, framed by the dramatic backdrop of the Remarkable, offer a picturesque setting that is sure to leave a lasting impression.

Entertainment

+ **Fergburger:**

Indulge in the legendary Fergburger, a Queenstown institution renowned for its mouthwatering gourmet burgers. Sink your teeth into juicy patties accompanied by an array of delectable toppings, all served in a vibrant and bustling atmosphere. Whether you opt for a classic beef burger or explore the vegetarian or vegan options, Fergburger is a must-visit culinary delight that has become an integral part of the Queenstown experience.

+ **Nightlife and Bars:**

Queenstown comes alive after dark, offering a vibrant nightlife scene with an array of bars and entertainment venues. From cozy pubs to stylish cocktail lounges, there is something to suit every taste. Enjoy live music, dance the night away, or simply unwind with a refreshing drink, soaking in the lively atmosphere that Queenstown's nightlife has to offer.

↓ Queenstown Gardens

Escape the hustle and bustle of the town center and retreat to the serene Queenstown Gardens. Take a leisurely stroll through the beautifully landscaped gardens, enjoy a picnic by the lake, or engage in recreational activities such as frisbee golf or tennis. The gardens provide a tranquil oasis where you can relax and appreciate the natural beauty that surrounds Queenstown.

Nelson

Situated at the top of New Zealand's South Island, Nelson is a city that immerses visitors in a world of creativity, outdoor recreation, and rich historical heritage. With its vibrant arts community, breath-taking landscapes, and significant historical sites, Nelson offers a unique and captivating experience. In this article, we embark on a journey through the distinct offerings of Nelson, exploring its thriving arts scene, diverse recreational opportunities, and fascinating heritage sites.

Arts

✦ World of Wearable Art (WOW) Museum

Step into a world where art and fashion collide at the World of Wearable Art Museum. This captivating museum showcases the extraordinary garments from the renowned annual WOW competition, where designers push the boundaries of creativity and innovation. Marvel at the intricate details, imaginative designs, and sheer ingenuity of wearable art creations. The museum also offers interactive displays and exhibits that provide insight into the creative process behind these incredible works of art.

✦ Suter Art Gallery

Immerse yourself in the vibrant arts community of Nelson at the Suter Art Gallery. Housed in a beautifully restored historic building, the gallery features a diverse collection of local and national artwork, spanning a range of styles and mediums. Explore contemporary exhibitions, discover traditional Maori art, and admire works by celebrated New Zealand artists. The Suter Art Gallery also hosts regular events, workshops, and artist talks, providing opportunities to engage with the local art scene.

Founders Heritage Park

Experience the fusion of art, history, and culture at Founders Heritage Park. This living museum showcases the region's rich heritage through interactive displays, preserved historic buildings, and engaging exhibitions. Wander through the streets of a recreated 19th-century village, visit craft workshops, and witness artisans at work. The park also hosts regular events, including art and craft markets, concerts, and festivals, offering a vibrant glimpse into Nelson's cultural tapestry.

Recreation

Abel Tasman National Park:

Nature enthusiasts and adventure seekers will find paradise in the Abel Tasman National Park. Explore the park's pristine golden beaches, crystal-clear waters, and lush coastal forests. Take a kayaking excursion, hike along the renowned Abel Tasman Coast Track, or simply relax on the secluded beaches. With its stunning landscapes and abundant wildlife, the national park offers endless opportunities for outdoor recreation and unforgettable experiences.

- **Nelson Lakes National Park**

  Discover the awe-inspiring beauty of Nelson Lakes National Park, home to rugged mountains, tranquil lakes, and captivating alpine scenery. Embark on hiking trails that wind through native beech forests, marvel at the reflection of the Southern Alps in Lake Rotoiti, or indulge in fishing and boating activities. The park is a haven for outdoor enthusiasts, providing a tranquil retreat where you can connect with nature and immerse yourself in the region's natural wonders.

- **Tahunanui Beach**

  Unwind and soak up the sun at Tahunanui Beach, Nelson's popular coastal playground. Stretching along the picturesque Tasman Bay, this sandy beach offers a host of recreational activities. Take a refreshing dip in the sparkling waters, build sandcastles with the family, or enjoy beachside picnics. Tahunanui Beach is also home to a variety of amenities, including cafes, restaurants, and playgrounds, making it a perfect spot for a day of relaxation and seaside fun.

Heritage Sites

+ **Nelson Cathedral:**

A symbol of Nelson's rich heritage, the Nelson Cathedral stands as an architectural masterpiece. Admire the Gothic Revival-style design, intricate stained-glass windows, and ornate woodwork as you explore the cathedral's interior. Take a moment for reflection or attend one of the regular services or musical performances, immersing yourself in the spiritual and historical ambiance of this significant site.

+ **Broadgreen Historic House**

Step back in time at Broadgreen Historic House, a beautifully preserved heritage home that provides a glimpse into colonial life in Nelson. Wander through the elegant rooms, adorned with period furnishings, and learn about the history of the original occupants. The surrounding gardens, with their manicured lawns and vibrant blooms, offer a peaceful oasis where you can appreciate the serenity of yesteryear.

+ **Miyazu Japanese Garden:**

Embrace the tranquility and beauty of the Miyazu Japanese Garden, a serene sanctuary nestled within Queen's Gardens. Designed to celebrate Nelson's sister city's relationship with

Miyazu, Japan, this authentic garden features traditional Japanese landscaping, serene water features, and meticulously manicured bonsai trees. Take a peaceful stroll along the winding paths, find a moment of contemplation in the tea house, and immerse yourself in the harmony and serenity of this cultural treasure.

Dunedin

Perched on the south-eastern coast of New Zealand's South Island, Dunedin is a city that seamlessly blends stunning architectural wonders, diverse wildlife encounters, and rich cultural experiences. With its heritage buildings, unique wildlife encounters, and vibrant arts scene, Dunedin offers a wealth of knowledge and captivating experiences for visitors. In this article, we embark on a journey through the distinctive aspects of Dunedin, exploring its remarkable architecture, abundant wildlife, and immersive cultural encounters.

Architecture

↓ Dunedin Railway Station

Immerse yourself in the grandeur of Dunedin's architectural heritage at the Dunedin Railway Station, a masterpiece of Victorian and Edwardian design. Admire the intricately detailed facade, adorned with ornate tilework, stained glass windows, and an impressive clock tower. Step inside to explore the beautifully restored interior, featuring mosaic floors, carved woodwork, and a stunning stained-glass ceiling. The Dunedin Railway Station stands as a testament to the city's rich history and architectural splendour.

+ Larnach Castle

Discover the only castle in New Zealand at Larnach Castle, perched atop the picturesque Otago Peninsula. This imposing 19th-century mansion boasts stunning architecture, lush gardens, and panoramic views. Take a guided tour to learn about the castle's history and explore its opulent interiors, including the ballroom, luxurious bedrooms, and the breath-taking tower. Larnach Castle offers a glimpse into the opulent lifestyle of the Victorian era and provides a truly enchanting experience.

+ First Church of Otago

Step inside the First Church of Otago, a prominent example of Gothic Revival architecture in New Zealand. Marvel at the towering spire, intricate stonework, and breath-taking stained-glass windows that illuminate the interior. The church's rich history and serene ambiance make it an ideal place for quiet contemplation or attending a musical performance. The First Church of Otago is a testament to Dunedin's architectural prowess and spiritual heritage

Wildlife

✦ Royal Albatross Centre

Embark on a journey to the Otago Peninsula and witness the majesty of the royal albatross, the world's largest seabird. Visit the Royal Albatross Centre, where you can observe these magnificent creatures in their natural habitat. Take a guided tour and learn about their life cycle, conservation efforts, and the significance of the Otago Peninsula as a breeding ground. This unique wildlife encounter offers a rare opportunity to connect with these awe-inspiring birds.

✦ Penguin Place

Delve into the world of the rare and endangered yellow-eyed penguins at Penguin Place. Join a guided tour through the carefully crafted conservation reserve, providing a safe haven for these fascinating creatures. Observe the penguins in their natural habitat, learn about their behaviour and conservation challenges, and witness their return from their daily fishing trips. Penguin Place offers a truly immersive and educational wildlife experience that leaves a lasting impression.

✦ Orokonui Ecosanctuary

Venture into the Orokonui Ecosanctuary, a haven for native New Zealand wildlife and lush forest ecosystems. Take a walk through the sanctuary's well-maintained trails, keeping an eye out for rare bird species, including the kiwi and takahe. Explore the informative visitor centre, which offers insights into the conservation efforts and the unique biodiversity of the region. Orokonui Ecosanctuary provides a sanctuary where visitors can appreciate the importance of preserving New Zealand's natural heritage.

Cultural Experiences

✦ Otago Museum:

Immerse yourself in the rich cultural heritage of Dunedin at the Otago Museum. Explore fascinating exhibits that showcase the natural history, art, and Maori heritage of the region. Engage with interactive displays, marvel at the diverse collection of artifacts, and learn about the cultural significance of Dunedin and its surrounding areas. The Otago

Museum offers an enriching and educational experience that celebrates the rich tapestry of the city's cultural heritage.

Dunedin Street Art Trail

Embark on a self-guided tour of Dunedin's vibrant street art scene. Wander through the streets to discover a diverse array of murals, sculptures, and installations that adorn the city's walls. Each artwork tells a unique story, reflecting the spirit and creativity of Dunedin's artistic community. The Street Art Trail provides a dynamic and ever-evolving cultural experience, showcasing the city's commitment to public art and expression.

Toitū Otago Settlers Museum

Step back in time and delve into the history of Dunedin and its early settlers at the Toitū Otago Settlers Museum. Explore the interactive exhibits, which bring to life the stories of the pioneers who shaped the region. From the Gold Rush era to the experiences of Maori and Pacific Islanders, the museum provides a comprehensive insight into the city's diverse cultural heritage. Engage with multimedia displays, authentic artifacts, and immersive reconstructions that transport you to the pas

Toitū Otago Settlers Museum

CHAPTER SEVEN

Discovering Natural Wonders

South Island, New Zealand, is a treasure trove of natural wonders, offering a captivating blend of awe-inspiring landscapes, diverse ecosystems, and unique geological formations. From towering mountains and serene fjords to pristine lakes and ancient glaciers, South Island's natural beauty is nothing short of extraordinary. In this article, we embark on an immersive journey, exploring the remarkable wonders that grace this remarkable region, leaving us in awe of the power and magnificence of nature.

Fiordland National Park

Fiordland National Park is not only a place of ethereal beauty but also holds deep historical significance. The fjords, including the famous Milford Sound and Doubtful Sound, were formed through the relentless carving of glaciers over thousands of years. However, the rich history of the park is also intertwined with the Maori people, who have inhabited the region for centuries. The Maori name for Milford Sound, "Piopiotahi," carries the legend of a bird's search for its lost love, symbolizing the deep spiritual connection between the Maori and the land. Exploring the fjords not only unveils breath-taking natural landscapes but also offers an opportunity to appreciate the cultural and historical heritage of the Maori people.

Stunning Landscapes

⊥ Majestic Fiords: Carved by Glaciers

Fiordland National Park is famous for its magnificent fiords, including the world-renowned Milford Sound, Doubtful Sound, and Dusky Sound. These fiords were carved by glaciers over millions of years, resulting in dramatic, steep-sided valleys that plunge into the deep, dark waters. Towering cliffs, adorned with cascading waterfalls and lush greenery, create an otherworldly atmosphere. Exploring the fiords by boat or kayak provides an opportunity to witness the sheer scale of these natural wonders, as well as encounter the rich biodiversity that thrives in these pristine environments.

⊥ Towering Peaks: The Southern Alps

The park is home to the majestic Southern Alps, which dominate the skyline and add to the breath-taking landscapes of Fiordland National Park. With peaks like Mitre Peak, Mount Tutoko, and Mount Christina, the mountains offer a stunning backdrop to the fiords and valleys. Snow-capped and rugged, these peaks create a sense of grandeur and awe. Hiking trails allow adventurers to immerse themselves in the alpine wonderland, offering panoramic views of the surrounding valleys, forests, and waterways. The towering peaks of Fiordland National Park are a testament to the dynamic geological forces that shaped this remarkable landscape.

⊹ Pristine Lakes: Mirror-like Reflections

Fiordland National Park boasts several pristine lakes that reflect the surrounding landscapes like shimmering mirrors. Lake Te Anau and Lake Manapouri, the largest lakes in the park, exude tranquility and provide a serene setting. The calm waters mirror the majestic mountains, lush forests, and clear skies, creating captivating reflections that enhance the visual beauty of the region. These lakes offer opportunities for boating, kayaking, and fishing, allowing visitors to immerse themselves in the serene ambiance while appreciating the unspoiled natural surroundings.

⊹ Ancient Rainforests: Verdant Canopies

The park's ancient rainforests add an enchanting element to its stunning landscapes. These primeval forests, rich in biodiversity, are home to towering trees such as the majestic rimu, towering kahikatea, and ancient totara. The forest floors are carpeted with vibrant ferns, mosses, and an array of delicate understory plants. Exploring the rainforests is like stepping into a prehistoric world, where the sights, sounds, and scents transport visitors to a bygone era. Native bird species, including the melodious tui and the elusive kiwi, can be spotted and heard among the dense foliage, adding to the ethereal atmosphere of these ancient ecosystems.

Waterways

Fiordland National Park, nestled in the southwestern corner of New Zealand's South Island, is renowned for its awe-inspiring waterways. Carved by ancient glaciers over millions of years, these pristine fiords and lakes create a majestic landscape that captivates visitors from around the world. Embarking on a journey through the waterways of Fiordland National Park offers a unique and unforgettable experience in the heart of the untouched wilderness.

✦ Fiords: Nature's Masterpieces

Fiords are the iconic gems of Fiordland National Park, and the park boasts some of the most famous and beautiful examples in the world, including Milford Sound, Doubtful Sound, and Dusky Sound. These dramatic waterways are carved by glaciers, resulting in steep-sided valleys that extend deep into the Tasman Sea. Towering cliffs, draped in lush rainforests, rise dramatically from the dark waters, creating a truly majestic sight. Exploring the fiords by boat or kayak allows you to witness cascading waterfalls, encounter playful seals, and experience the tranquility of this untouched wilderness.

⊥ Lakes: Mirror-Like Serenity

Fiordland National Park is also home to an array of pristine lakes that reflect the surrounding landscapes with breathtaking beauty. Lake Te Anau, the largest lake in the park, offers a serene escape with its crystal-clear waters and mountainous backdrop. Lake Manapouri, known for its tranquility and untouched wilderness, is often hailed as one of New Zealand's most beautiful lakes. These mirror-like lakes provide opportunities for boating, kayaking, and fishing, allowing visitors to immerse themselves in the serenity of the surroundings and appreciate the unspoiled natural beauty.

Waterfalls: Nature's Cascading Spectacles

The waterways of Fiordland National Park are adorned with numerous cascading waterfalls that add to the enchantment of the landscape. The iconic Stirling Falls in Milford Sound plunges from a height of 155 meters (509 feet), creating a breathtaking spectacle. Bowen Falls, also in Milford Sound, is another impressive waterfall, cascading gracefully into the fiord. The mesmerizing sight and sound of these waterfalls evoke a sense of wonder and remind us of the power and beauty of nature.

Marine Life and Wildlife Encounters

The waterways of Fiordland National Park are not only visually stunning but also teeming with marine life and wildlife. Pods of dolphins frolic in the fiords, often playfully approaching boats and enchanting visitors with their agility. Fur seals bask on rocky outcrops, while rare species such as the Fiordland crested penguin and the Hector's dolphin call this region home. Exploring the waterways provides opportunities for remarkable wildlife encounters, allowing you to witness these creatures in their natural habitat and appreciate the park's ecological diversity.

✦ Pristine Wilderness and Serenity

What sets the waterways of Fiordland National Park apart is the sense of pristine wilderness and serenity they evoke. With limited human presence, these waterways offer an escape into untouched nature, allowing visitors to disconnect from the outside world and immerse themselves in the tranquility of their surroundings. The silence, interrupted only by the sounds of nature, creates a profound connection with the environment and a deep appreciation for the beauty and fragility of this extraordinary place

Milford Sound

Milford Sound, nestled within Fiordland National Park in New Zealand's South Island, is renowned for its awe-inspiring beauty and pristine wilderness. Embarking on a cruise or scenic flight through Milford Sound offers a unique and unforgettable experience, immersing you in the breath-taking grandeur of this iconic natural wonder.

Cruises and Scenic Flights

Cruising through Milford Sound is the most popular way to experience its magnificence. Boarding a boat, you'll venture deep into the heart of the fjord, surrounded by towering cliffs adorned with lush rainforests. As you navigate the tranquil waters, cascading waterfalls, such as the iconic Stirling Falls and Bowen Falls, create a spectacle of natural beauty. Keep an eye out for the playful dolphins that often accompany the boats, and if you're lucky, you may even spot seals basking on rocky outcrops. The serenity and awe-inspiring scenery of Milford Sound will leave you captivated throughout the journey.

For a truly remarkable perspective, taking a scenic flight over Milford Sound is an unparalleled experience. Soar high above the towering peaks and deep valleys, gazing down at the dramatic landscape below. From above, the immense scale of the fiord is revealed, showcasing its sheer cliffs and winding waterways. Marvel at the sight of cascading waterfalls as they plunge into the fiord, and witness the intricate network of lakes and rivers that feed into the Sound. Scenic flights provide an extraordinary opportunity to appreciate the pristine wilderness and grasp the true magnitude of Milford Sound's natural beauty.

No journey through Milford Sound would be complete without beholding the majestic Mitre Peak. Rising dramatically from the water to a height of 1,692 meters (5,551 feet), this iconic landmark stands as a symbol of the region's grandeur. Its distinctive shape, resembling a bishop's miter, adds to the allure of the fjord. Whether you witness Mitre Peak from a cruise boat or a scenic flight, its commanding presence is a highlight of any visit to Milford Sound.

Milford Sound is renowned for its tranquillity and the sense of untouched wilderness it exudes. As you cruise or fly through the fiord, you'll be enveloped by a sense of serenity and captivated by the unspoiled natural wonders around you. The pristine waters, the towering cliffs cloaked in verdant foliage, and the absence of human development create an atmosphere of profound tranquillity. Embrace the opportunity to disconnect from the outside world and immerse yourself in the raw beauty of Milford Sound.

Doubtful Sound

Doubtful Sound, situated in the pristine wilderness of Fiordland National Park in New Zealand's South Island, is a breathtaking destination that offers an abundance of natural wonders and thrilling adventures. From its untouched wilderness to its diverse wildlife, hiking trails, and exhilarating activities, Doubtful Sound provides an immersive experience for nature lovers and adventure enthusiasts alike.

Wilderness and Wildlife

Doubtful Sound's wilderness is a captivating landscape of ancient rainforests, cascading waterfalls, and towering cliffs that rise dramatically from the dark waters. As you venture deep into the fiord, you'll be surrounded by an untouched environment that transports you to a realm of pristine beauty. The serenity of the sound allows you to truly connect with nature and appreciate its magnificence.

The sound is also home to a diverse range of wildlife. Keep your eyes peeled for the playful dolphins that often swim alongside boats, offering delightful companionship during your journey. Encounter seals basking on rocks, and marvel at the flight of native birds, including the majestic Fiordland crested penguin and the elusive New Zealand falcon. Wildlife encounters in Doubtful Sound are an extraordinary opportunity to witness the richness and diversity of the region's ecosystem.

Hiking Trails and Adventure Activities

Doubtful Sound is surrounded by a network of hiking trails that allow you to explore the region's breathtaking landscapes on foot. The renowned Lake Manapouri Track takes you on a journey through lush forests, offering panoramic views of Lake

Manapouri and its surrounding mountains. For more adventurous hikers, the challenging Dusky Track rewards with its remote wilderness and rugged terrain. These hiking trails provide an immersive experience, allowing you to embrace the tranquillity of the surroundings and witness the pristine beauty up close.

Embarking on a kayaking or boating adventure in Doubtful Sound is a remarkable way to experience the grandeur of the fiord. Glide through the tranquil waters, surrounded by towering cliffs and verdant rainforests. Paddle alongside waterfalls and explore hidden coves and inlets. The peacefulness of kayaking allows for a more intimate connection with the surroundings, while boating offers a broader perspective of the awe-inspiring landscape. Whether by kayak or boat, these waterborne adventures provide an unforgettable encounter with the natural wonders of Doubtful Sound.

For those seeking an adventure on the water, fishing trips and wildlife cruises in Doubtful Sound offer unique experiences. Try your hand at fishing in these abundant waters, where you may have the chance to catch species such as blue cod or sea-run trout. Alternatively, join a wildlife cruise to further explore the sound, taking you closer to marine and birdlife. Expert guides provide insights into the region's natural history and ecology, enriching your understanding of the area's diverse wildlife.

5. Overnight Cruises and Stargazing:

To fully immerse yourself in the magic of Doubtful Sound, consider an overnight cruise. Spend the night aboard a comfortable vessel, surrounded by the serenity of the fiord. Wake up to the gentle sounds of nature and witness the beauty of sunrise over the water. During the evening, stargazing becomes a mesmerizing experience, as Doubtful Sound is part of the UNESCO Dark Sky Reserve. Marvel at the celestial wonders above, far away from city lights, and appreciate the tranquility of this pristine wilderness.

CHAPTER EIGHT

Itineraries and Day Trips

This 10-day itinerary offers a glimpse into the diverse beauty and adventure that South Island has to offer. From coastal wonders to majestic glaciers, and pristine national parks to adrenaline-pumping activities, your journey through South Island will be filled with unforgettable experiences and breath-taking landscapes at every turn.

South Island Highlights Itinerary

10-Day Itinerary: Exploring the Highlights of South Island

10-Day Journey

Day 1

Arrive in Christchurch Start your South Island adventure by arriving in Christchurch, the largest city on the island. Spend the day exploring the city's vibrant arts scene, botanical gardens, and unique architecture. Visit the Canterbury Museum to learn about the region's history and culture.

Day 2

Christchurch to Kaikoura Embark on a scenic drive from Christchurch to Kaikoura, a coastal town renowned for its abundant marine life. Take a whale-watching tour or swim with dolphins. Enjoy freshly caught seafood at one of the local restaurants and soak in the stunning coastal views.

Day 3

Kaikoura to Abel Tasman National Park Head north to Abel Tasman National Park, famous for its golden beaches, turquoise waters, and lush forests. Spend the day hiking the picturesque coastal tracks or take a guided sea kayaking tour to explore the park's pristine coastline.

Day 4

Abel Tasman National Park to Punakaiki Drive south along the rugged West Coast to Punakaiki, known for its unique Pancake Rocks and blowholes. Explore the Pancake Rocks Walkway, where you can witness the dramatic waves crashing against the limestone formations. Experience the wild beauty of the West Coast as you settle in for the night.

Day 5

Punakaiki to Franz Josef Glacier Continue your journey south to Franz Josef Glacier, one of New Zealand's most iconic natural wonders. Take a guided glacier hike or scenic helicopter flight to witness the stunning ice formations and rugged alpine landscapes. Relax in the hot pools nestled amidst the rainforest.

Day 6

Franz Josef Glacier to Wanaka Drive through breath-taking mountain scenery to the picturesque town of Wanaka. Enjoy a stroll along the lakefront or hike up Mount Iron for panoramic views of the surrounding area. Don't miss the famous Wanaka Tree, a solitary willow tree standing in the lake.

Day 7

Wanaka to Queenstown Travel from Wanaka to Queenstown, known as the adventure capital of New Zealand. Experience thrilling activities like bungee jumping, jet boating, or skydiving. Take a scenic gondola ride to the top of Bob's Peak for stunning views of Lake Wakatipu and the Remarkable Mountain range.

Day 8

Queenstown and Milford Sound Embark on a day trip to the majestic Milford Sound, often called the Eighth Wonder of the World. Cruise through the stunning fiord, surrounded by towering cliffs and cascading waterfalls. Keep an eye out for dolphins, seals, and penguins. Return to Queenstown in the evening.

Day 9

Queenstown to Mount Cook National Park Drive to Mount Cook National Park, home to New Zealand's highest peak, Aoraki/Mount Cook. Take a scenic hike or join a guided tour to explore the alpine beauty of the park. Visit the Sir Edmund Hillary Alpine Centre to learn about the history of mountaineering in the region.

Day 10

Mount Cook National Park to Christchurch On your final day, make your way back to Christchurch. Along the way, stop at Lake Tekapo to admire its turquoise waters and visit the iconic Church of the Good Shepherd. Arrive in Christchurch with time to explore any attractions you may have missed on your first day.

Day Trip to Abel Tasman National Park

A day trip to Abel Tasman National Park on New Zealand's South Island is the perfect choice. Renowned for its golden beaches, turquoise waters, and lush forests, Abel Tasman National Park offers a captivating experience that will leave you in awe of its pristine beauty.

To begin your day, drive to the park's entrance or catch a scenic water taxi from nearby towns such as Marahau or Kaiteriteri. Once inside the park, a variety of options will allow you to make the most of your day:

1. **Coastal Walk**

   Embark on a portion of the renowned Abel Tasman Coast Track, a stunning trail that winds along the park's picturesque coastline. Choose a section that aligns with your fitness level and time constraints. The track unveils breathtaking vistas, secluded bays, and opportunities to spot native wildlife along the way. Marvel at the turquoise waters and golden sands as you immerse yourself in this coastal paradise.

2. **Kayaking Adventure**

Rent a kayak or join a guided kayaking tour to explore the park's coastal wonders from the water. Paddle through crystal-clear waters, gliding past hidden coves and rocky outcrops. Admire the rugged cliffs and marvel at the marine life that inhabits these pristine waters. Keep a keen eye out for playful seals and dolphins that often make appearances, adding to the magic of your journey.

3. **Water Taxi Excursion**

   Opt for a water taxi excursion, which allows you to hop on and off at various points along the coast. These convenient services grant you the flexibility to explore different sections of the park and enjoy leisurely walks on secluded beaches. Relax on pristine shores, take a refreshing swim, or simply bask in the tranquility of your surroundings.

4. **Wildlife Spotting**

   Abel Tasman National Park is home to a variety of native bird species, including the playful and colorful New Zealand fantail (piwakawaka) and the vibrant bellbird (korimako). Keep your senses attuned to these feathered inhabitants as you traverse the park's trails or relax on the beaches. If fortune smiles upon you, you may also catch sight of fur seals basking on the rocks or dolphins frolicking in the coastal waters.

5. **Picnic and Beach Time**

Take a respite from your adventures and relish a leisurely picnic on one of the park's picturesque beaches. Pack a delectable lunch and seek out a peaceful spot to unwind, enveloped by the natural beauty of Abel Tasman National Park. Listen to the gentle lapping of the waves, feel the soft sand between your toes, and appreciate the serenity of this coastal paradise.

A Scenic Drive to Mount Cook National Park

Embarking on a scenic drive to Mount Cook National Park in New Zealand's South Island is an invitation to immerse yourself in the awe-inspiring beauty of the alpine landscape. The journey to this iconic park takes you through breath-taking vistas, picturesque towns, and a sense of serenity that only the mountains can offer.

As you set off on your drive, the road winds through lush farmlands and rolling hills, gradually revealing glimpses of snow-capped peaks in the distance. The drive itself becomes part of the experience, with every turn offering a new and more stunning panorama.

Along the way, you'll pass through charming towns such as Twizel, where you can take a moment to appreciate the tranquillity and rural charm of the region. Consider stopping for a coffee or a meal, or simply stretch your legs and breathe in the fresh alpine air.

As you continue your journey, the grandeur of the Southern Alps begins to dominate the horizon. Mount Cook, New Zealand's highest peak, majestically emerges, towering above the surrounding peaks. Its snow-clad summit captures the imagination and serves as a beacon, drawing you closer to its alpine splendour.

The road leads you to the village of Mount Cook, nestled at the base of the mountain. Here, you'll find a range of activities and experiences that allow you to immerse yourself in the park's natural wonders. Take a guided hike or join a scenic flight to witness the grandeur of the Tasman Glacier, the longest glacier in New Zealand. Marvel at the turquoise waters of Lake Pukaki, which reflect the surrounding peaks, creating a mesmerizing spectacle of colours.

As you explore Mount Cook National Park, you'll be enchanted by the pristine alpine environment. Towering peaks, deep valleys, and glacial lakes paint a picture of untouched wilderness. The crisp air, the silence broken only by the sound of nature, and the sense of serenity envelop you, providing a true escape from the hustle and bustle of everyday life.

Whether you embark on a challenging hike or simply bask in the tranquillity of the park, the journey to Mount Cook National Park offers a profound connection with nature. The raw beauty of the landscape will leave an indelible impression, reminding you of the incredible power and majesty of the mountains.

As the sun begins to set, casting a warm glow on the peaks, you may find yourself yearning to stay a little longer, to witness the mountains in different light and seasons. Mount Cook National Park beckons adventurers and nature enthusiasts alike, offering an unforgettable experience that will forever hold a special place in your heart.

Exploring the Marlborough Wine Region

The Marlborough Wine Region, located in the north-eastern part of New Zealand's South Island, is a true paradise for wine lovers. Celebrated for its world-class Sauvignon Blanc, this region offers a captivating blend of picturesque landscapes, vineyard-dotted valleys, and award-winning wineries. Embark on a journey through the Marlborough Wine Region to savour exquisite wines, indulge in culinary delights, and immerse yourself in the vibrant wine culture.

✦ Wine Tastings and Vineyard Tours:

Begin your exploration by visiting some of the renowned wineries in Marlborough. Experience the diversity of flavors and aromas as you indulge in tastings of their exceptional Sauvignon Blanc, as well as other varietals like Chardonnay, Pinot Noir, and Riesling. Take guided vineyard tours to gain insights into the winemaking process, from grape to bottle. Learn about the region's unique terroir and the passion that goes into crafting these exceptional wines.

Cellar Door Experiences

Delve deeper into the wine culture by visiting the cellar doors of Marlborough's wineries. Engage with knowledgeable staff who are passionate about sharing their expertise and stories. Expand your palate as you sample a variety of wines, discovering new favorites along the way. Take the opportunity to purchase bottles to enjoy later or as souvenirs to remind you of your time in this wine paradise.

Culinary Delights:

Pair your wine tastings with delectable culinary experiences. Many wineries in Marlborough boast exceptional restaurants and cafes, offering gourmet dishes that perfectly complement the wines. Indulge in a leisurely lunch showcasing local produce, artisan cheeses, and freshly caught seafood. Immerse yourself in the region's farm-to-table philosophy and enjoy the gastronomic delights that enhance your wine journey.

Cycling the Marlborough Wine Trail

For an active and immersive experience, consider cycling the Marlborough Wine Trail. Rent a bike and meander through the vineyards, taking in the breath-taking scenery at your own pace. Pedal from one winery to another, stopping for tastings and enjoying the fresh air as you explore this picturesque region. The wine trail allows you to appreciate the beauty of the landscape while enjoying the wines that have made Marlborough famous.

Marlborough Sounds and Wine Cruises

Extend your wine exploration beyond the vineyards by taking a wine cruise through the stunning Marlborough Sounds. Relax on board a boat as you sail through the tranquil waters, surrounded by majestic landscapes. Sip on local wines while marvelling at the coastal beauty and the unique interplay of land and sea. Learn about the region's history and enjoy the tranquillity of the sounds as you indulge in a truly unique wine experience.

Marlborough Wine and Food Festival:

If you have the opportunity, plan your visit during the Marlborough Wine and Food Festival, held annually in February. This vibrant event showcases the best of the region's wines, culinary delights, and live entertainment. Immerse yourself in the festive atmosphere, mingle with winemakers, and savour the flavor of Marlborough in one unforgettable celebration.

Coastal Adventure

The South Island of New Zealand is a haven for coastal adventurers, offering a diverse range of experiences that blend the power of the ocean with the allure of the shoreline. From rugged cliffs to pristine beaches, marine wildlife encounters to thrilling water sports, a coastal adventure in South Island promises endless excitement and unforgettable memories

Kaikoura and Wildlife Encounters

Kaikoura, a coastal town nestled on the eastern shores of New Zealand's South Island, is a destination renowned for its remarkable wildlife encounters. Surrounded by the rich marine environment of the Pacific Ocean and bordered by the mighty

Kaikoura Ranges, this unique location offers a captivating blend of natural beauty and close encounters with marine creatures. Immerse yourself in the wonders of Kaikoura and embark on unforgettable wildlife experiences that will leave you in awe.

✦ Whale-Watching

Kaikoura is world-famous for its exceptional whale-watching opportunities. Join a whale-watching tour and venture out into the ocean to witness the awe-inspiring sight of these magnificent creatures. Kaikoura is particularly known for its encounters with sperm whales, the largest toothed whales on Earth. Marvel at their massive size as they breach the surface, and listen to the mesmerizing sound of their blows. With knowledgeable guides on board, you'll learn about the whales' behaviour, migration patterns, and conservation efforts to protect these gentle giants.

* **Dolphin Encounters:**

In addition to whales, Kaikoura is home to a thriving population of dusky dolphins. Swim or kayak alongside these playful and acrobatic creatures as they frolic in the pristine waters. Experience the joy of interacting with dolphins in their natural habitat, witnessing their impressive flips, spins, and leaps. The sense of connection and pure exhilaration that comes from these encounters is truly unforgettable.

Fur Seal Colony

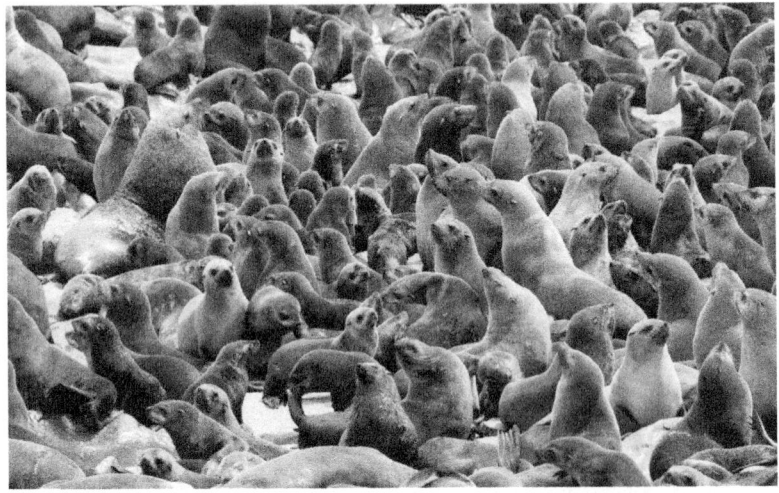

Visit the Ohau Point Seal Colony, s a short drive from Kaikoura, to observe a thriving colony of New Zealand fur seals. Watch as these curious and charismatic animals lounge on the rocks, play in the shallows, and interact with each other. The colony provides a fantastic opportunity for up-close encounters and remarkable photography. Observe the seals' behaviours and learn about their life cycle and importance in the coastal ecosystem.

⊹ Albatross Encounters

Kaikoura's coastal location also offers the chance to spot magnificent albatrosses, the world's largest seabirds, soaring gracefully above the ocean. Join a scenic flight or head to the Kaikoura Peninsula to witness these majestic birds in flight. With their impressive wingspans and effortless gliding, albatrosses create a spectacle that showcases the beauty and grace of nature.

✈ Marine Wildlife Cruises

Take a leisurely cruise along Kaikoura's coast to fully appreciate the abundance of marine life. These cruises provide opportunities to encounter a variety of species, including seals, dolphins, seabirds, and even the occasional pod of orca whales. Enjoy the commentary from knowledgeable guides who share insights about the region's wildlife, ecology, and conservation efforts. Capture stunning photographs and create memories that will last a lifetime.

⭐ Coastal Walks and Scenic Views

Kaikoura offers a range of coastal walks and viewpoints that provide breath-taking panoramas of the surrounding landscape. Take a stroll along the Kaikoura Peninsula Walkway to enjoy sweeping vistas of the ocean, mountains, and wildlife. Capture postcard-worthy photographs of the rugged coastline and the meeting point of land and sea. These walks offer an opportunity to connect with nature and appreciate the stunning beauty that Kaikoura has to offer.

Printed in Great Britain
by Amazon

45013554R00119